The Best Decision I Ever Made

The Best Decision I Ever Made

Stories of Jesus Changing Lives

Introduced by Rob Parsons

Hodder & Stoughton
LONDON SYDNEY AUCKLAND

Copyright © 1999 by the contributors
Introduction copyright © 1999 by Rob Parsons

First published in Great Britain in 1999

British Library Cataloguing in Publication Data
A record for this book is available from the British Library

ISBN 0 340 72233 9

Typeset by Avon Dataset Ltd, Bidford-on-Avon, Warks

Printed and bound in Great Britain by
Clays Ltd, St Ives plc

Hodder & Stoughton Ltd
A Division of Hodder Headline PLC
338 Euston Road
London NW1 3BH

Contents

List of Contributors

Born and brought up in Montrose, on the east coast of Scotland, **Lesley Bilinda** is now working as a Tutor at All Nations Christian College in Hertfordshire and runs the Charles Bilinda Memorial Trust. She was a Tear Fund health worker on leave from Rwanda when the killing began. Her husband, Rwandan pastor Charles Bilinda, had stayed behind. She never heard from him again, and tells her heart-rending story in *The Colour of Darkness*.

From the world of television to the streets of Brazil, **Sarah de Carvalho** tells her remarkable story in the international bestseller, *The Street Children of Brazil*. Through an extraordinary series of events, Sarah left her glittering career in television and film and founded the Happy Child Mission with her husband Joao.

Fiona Castle is the widow of Roy Castle, the popular TV entertainer, and a mother of four children. She is the author of *Rainbows Through the Rain – An Anthology of Hope* in which she shares with us her sources of inspiration.

Adviser in Evangelism to the Archbishops of Canterbury and York and established Bible teacher, **Michael Green** is the author of numerous books including *Evangelism for Amateurs*, *The Empty Cross of Jesus* and *I Believe in the Holy Spirit*. He is married to Rosemary Green, a teacher at conferences of clergy and laity alike.

Michele Guinness is a freelance journalist, broadcaster and public relations consultant. Raised in a Jewish family and married to an Anglican clergyman, she has worked extensively in radio and television and published a number of books including *Child of the Covenant*, *Promised Land*, *A Little Kosher Seasoning*, *Is God Good for Women?* and *The Guinness Spirit*.

Minister at Westminster Chapel, London, **R. T. Kendall** is a much-loved writer and speaker. He is the author of numerous bestselling works including *The Anointing*, *The Gift of Giving* and *Thorn in the Flesh*. He is well-known for his Bible readings at Spring Harvest and Keswick.

Jennifer Rees Larcombe is a mother of six and the author of many popular books including *Beyond Healing*, *Where Have You Gone, God?* and *Unexpected Healing*. From her own experience of suffering and with the wisdom of Christians down the ages, she offers comfort and hope to all those who feel distant from God.

Alister McGrath is Principal of Wycliffe Hall, Oxford, and Professor of Systematic Theology at Regent College, Vancouver. He is consultant editor of *Christianity Today* and the author of numerous books including *To Know And Serve God – A Biography of James I. Packer*, *Theology for Amateurs* and *The Journey*.

J. I. Packer is an eminent theologian. Currently Professor of Theology at Regent College, Vancouver, he is a bestselling author whose many books include *God Has Spoken*, *Knowing God*, *Life in the Spirit* and *A Passion for Faithfulness*.

David Pawson has an itinerant ministry to church leaders in the UK and overseas. He is the author of numerous books, including *The Normal Christian Birth*, *Once Saved, Always Saved?*, *Word and Spirit Together* and *The Road to Hell*.

Julie Sheldon was formerly a ballet dancer, but was stricken with the crippling disease dystonia. Since her miraculous recovery, she has devoted herself to evangelistic speaking events and to her family. She is the author of *The Blessing of Tears* and *Dancer Off Her Feet*, which recounts her story.

Colin Urquhart is the Director of Kingdom Faith Ministries. He has an international teaching ministry, and is a much-loved leader and author. His bestselling works include *Anything You Ask*, *From Mercy to Majesty* and *Listen and Live*.

Introduction

If I close my eyes I can imagine I am there again. The date is August 1961, and I am in a muddy field at Oxwich on the Gower peninsula, Wales. Neither of my parents went to church but they were keen that I attend and sent me to the little 'Gospel Hall' on the corner of our street. Each year that small church joined with dozens of others to organise a summer camp for boys. The days were spent playing football or swimming off the Gower coastline, but every evening tired teenagers would gather in a large tent to sing what would now be called 'worship songs' but were then called 'choruses', and to listen to somebody speak about the Christian faith.

And so it was that on a balmy August evening I found myself listening as Bill Lord told us about the God who had captured his heart. It was later that night in a small tent that one of the other helpers at the camp, Jack Whittington, carefully and with great sensitivity, helped a young man to express his need of Christ.

I have often gone back to the field where the event occurred; for me it is practically holy ground. One of the contributors in this book mentions that God not only saves us from our past but our futures. I sometimes wonder how different my 'future' would have been without that encounter with Christ. He has been, and is, my greatest friend. Somebody has said the way to know how much you love somebody or something is to imagine it gone forever. There have been times when my love for him has seemed almost to have died. These were not so much periods of doubt, although I have certainly known that, but of what somebody once called in a marriage 'a creeping separateness'. These have been some of the most miserable times of my life. I cannot live without him.

But I am meant to be introducing this wonderful book, not adding to it! Forgive me. It's just that as I have read the accounts of these men and women my heart has been touched and it has been impossible for me not to dwell a little on the Christ who also called me all those years ago. To read the stories contained in this book has been, for me, a sheer delight. Some of the contributors have been heroes of mine for many years; writing this introduction has made me feel like a first-form schoolboy penning a reference for the headmaster!

I remember the first time I heard David Pawson preach. I felt as if somebody had taken the Bible and made it as relevant as the daily newspaper. He made the Gospels live for me. And I recall Dr R. T. Kendall saying to me one day, 'Rob – *God is for you*.' What a revelation that was to me. I had spent much of my life trying to earn God's love and then as R. T. spoke it dawned on me, 'He is for me when I feel close to him and when he seems far away, he is for me when I succeed and when I fail, he is for me when my head is filled with certainty and when my heart is filled with doubt, he is for me when I share my faith with thousands and when I deny him. God is *for* me.'

I recall reading Michael Green's *Man Alive* when I was in college and realising that I could believe without committing intellectual suicide. And Jim Packer: I first read his classic book, *Knowing God*, when I was a young man. The edition I have in my study is old and dog-eared. On the back cover a young Anglican called John Stott says of Dr Packer, 'The truth he handles fires the heart.'

As I have read this book I have found some new heroes. Who could not be moved to tears by Lesley Bilinda's story of the horrors of the conflict in Rwanda and the tragic death of her husband? And I defy you to walk the streets of Brazil with Sarah de Carvalho without wanting to cradle one of the street children in your arms.

But in truth I have been touched by every one of these accounts. At times I have felt as if these men and women have allowed me into their very souls. I believe that you, too, will be blessed as you read. But you may find, as I did, that at the end you will be impressed not so much with famous names as with *a* name. I sensed that Jesus himself spoke to me as I read this book. I am quite sure that each of the contributors would want no less for each of you. May God bless you as you begin *The Best Decision I Ever Made*.

Rob Parsons

1

'If this is the way you want it, God'

Fiona Castle

On 25 February 1975 God challenged me with these words from Revelation 3:20: 'Look! Here I stand at the door and knock. If you hear me calling and open the door, I will come in, and we will share a meal as friends' (New Living Translation). Those words changed my life in the most amazing and miraculous way on a day when I had given up on life – I was desperate and knew that something had to happen if I was to survive.

Sometime later I reread those words but I started at the beginning of the letter to the church in Laodicea and I realised that it could have been written about me!

I know all the things you do, that you are neither hot nor cold. I wish you were one or the other! But since you are like luke warm water, I will spit you out of my mouth! You say 'I am rich. I have everything I want. I don't need a thing!' And you don't realize that you are wretched and miserable and poor and blind and naked. I advise you to buy gold from me – gold that has been purified by fire. Then you will be rich. And also buy white garments so you will not be shamed by your nakedness. And buy ointment for your eyes so you will be able to see. I am the one who corrects and disciplines everyone I love. Be diligent and turn from your indifference.

(Revelation 3:15–19, New Living Translation)

I was 'happily' married to a successful show business entertainer. We had four beautiful, healthy children. We lacked nothing in material possessions. We had a lovely home, a close family; in all an idyllic situation.

The trouble was, I felt my life was falling apart. I had suffered on and off with depression for several years, which could have been attributed to self-pity. I sensed that I was expected to live the beautiful life, but instead I was lonely, depressed and I felt trapped in my own home. I felt guilty. How could someone who had everything be so miserable and feel so empty inside?

Roy was away from home much of the time, travelling abroad as well as countrywide, leaving me of course to cope with all that went on within the home. This should not have been a problem. I loved being a homemaker and I took pride in doing the job really well. I understood the hazards of show business, having also been in the theatre before we were married. I had chosen to give up my career so that I could tour with Roy. Initially he was working as much in the United States as he was at home so I knew that if I pursued my career, based in London, we'd see very little of each other. I also loved the prospect of running a home, and with four children whom I adored, one could say that my life should have been complete.

However, I was somewhat of a perfectionist and everything had to run like clockwork in order for me to feel that I was succeeding. This necessitated often working halfway through the night to keep everything in order. This didn't help my equilibrium or depression and added to my sense of failure. My self-esteem was at rock bottom.

During this time our marriage was going through a very difficult patch. I only had myself to blame for this, because Roy was a very loving, tolerant and long-suffering husband, happy if everyone around him was happy. Unfortunately my behaviour was causing enormous tension between us.

Because of the pressure of Roy's work, he was very focussed on (and sometimes blinkered by) what he had to do – scripts to write, scripts to learn, orchestrations to arrange – I in turn was totally wrapped up in organising the family. We were running on parallel lines but not interacting or supporting one another as we might have done. I was so worried about my own pressures and problems, I didn't notice his.

This situation was not constant, but over a period of time it became more frequent. I think Roy thought that by being at home I had the easy task and, as he put it, 'the best bite of the cherry', whereas I would be quite jealous when he would phone me late at night after a show to tell me it had been great and then go on to tell me who he was with and where they were and what they were eating! There'd be a stony silence, while I considered the leftover fish-fingers I'd eaten for supper. It would invariably end up with one of us slamming the phone down on the other! Communication was not good between us.

Communication is so important in a marriage and often it is the first thing that breaks down, as pressures and stresses arise and couples are not willing to listen to each other. When children are added to the equation, the problems multiply. I now know how common these problems are; at the time I thought I was the only one!

If only we could drop our masks and be honest with one another, life would be so much simpler. I kept mine firmly in place because I thought if people knew the real me they wouldn't like what they saw. Instead I tried my best to please everyone and never liked to say no to people's requests for help. I wanted to be known as a coper – with hindsight I realise it was to bolster my self-esteem. Consequently I was on a treadmill, running fast but getting nowhere, but not wanting to stop, because I knew I wouldn't like what I saw if I looked at myself!

I remember my mother telling me that a mother is the pivot point of the home. If the mother is anxious, tense, irritable or bad-tempered it's not long before the whole family reflects that mood. I recognised this in my own home. The children were tense at times, not knowing how I would react or what sort of mother they would come home to. Much depended on my mood at the time, which did not help them feel secure. I was trying to be a good wife and mother and most of the time I felt an utter failure.

So, it was against this background that I got down on my knees in my bedroom one morning and cried out to God. 'God, if you're there at all,' I said, 'You've got to help me and you've got to help me now, because I've had it. I can't go on any longer.'

That's all. I didn't expect an answer but I knew something had to happen if I was to survive. I had tried everything I could think of to make life work for me but nothing changed me. This was a heart cry and God answered. 'I will answer them before they even call to me. While they are still talking to me about their needs, I will go ahead and answer their prayers!' (Isaiah 65:24, New Living Translation).

The phone rang. When I answered it, the person who was calling was a friend of my sister and I knew she was a Christian. 'Fiona,' she said, 'I've had you on my mind and had this sudden urge to phone you. I feel as if you and I need to meet and have a chat. I don't know why or what we'd chat about but come and have a coffee.'

Realising that this had to be God's way of answering my cry for help, I dropped everything and went round to see her. Because I didn't know Tamara very well at this time I didn't feel threatened by her and felt I could pour out my problems to her. She was a good listener and when I had finished she asked me a life-changing question. 'You know, Fiona, you think you're a Christian because you've always gone to church, but have you ever asked Jesus to come in and take over your life?'

'No' came the honest reply, 'I didn't realise I was supposed to.'

'Well, don't you think it's about time you did?'

'Yes.' We were in the room alone together and this wasn't the time to start making excuses, although I was a bit worried about the implications. Would it mean that I would have to give up things and try even harder to do the right thing? After all, I was already trying and failing miserably.

It was then she read those amazing words to me from Revelation, and I realised that Jesus had been knocking at the door of my heart for thirty-five years and I'd never invited him in. I had only paid him lip-service by singing hymns and saying my prayers but always held on tightly to the reins of my own life very firmly.

This was my moment. I asked Jesus to forgive me for the mess I'd made of my life, my family and my marriage. Then I asked him to take over – that's all – and he did! I experienced peace I never knew was possible. I can only describe it as having soothing oil poured all over and right through me, releasing all the tension inside. To my amazement I didn't fall apart as I let go of those reins. Jesus gave me back my life! He'd set me free from being what I thought I ought to be or what I thought others thought I ought to be and was giving me the opportunity to become what *he* wanted me to be. I went home knowing that I would face the same situations I'd faced before, but now I knew I had Jesus to help me. I didn't need to be afraid when things didn't go my way.

Although I didn't tell Roy what had happened, he told me later that he noticed straightaway that I was different. He didn't mention it either in case it didn't last!

The Bible came alive with meaning and relevance. I was amazed at all the things it said about marriage and raising families and even more amazed that when I put them into practice they worked. It took the pressure off me to conform to society's demands on me and the family. God had a plan and a pathway for my life. 'I will guide you along the best pathway for your life.

I will advise you and watch over you' (Psalm 32:8, New Living Translation). My prayer for my family became that God would show them the plans he had for their lives too. That continues to be my prayer for them today.

I am so grateful to God that this all happened while I still had time to make amends for the way I'd been so that our home became filled with noise and laughter – plenty of mistakes but with the guts to say sorry. In 1 Peter 3:11 we read, 'Strive for peace even if you have to run after it to catch it and hold it' (The Living Bible). I wanted my home to be a place where my children would want to bring their friends because there would always be a happy atmosphere. There were times when I had to 'run after it' because I couldn't bear unresolved strife or tension. Harmony was a priority for me.

Roy and I learned to appreciate one another again, with a real desire to meet each other's needs and to cherish each other. I had promised to 'cherish' on our wedding day. I had also promised to love and honour, for better, for worse, for richer, for poorer, in sickness and in health. We never know when we will be called to put that into practice. We never imagine the 'worse' or the 'sickness' when we are young and very much in love. I suppose we expect it will always be wonderful!

Jesus never said it would be easy. He said, 'Here on earth you will have many trials and sorrows. But take heart, because I have overcome the world' (John 16:33, New Living Translation). He didn't say, 'might', he said, 'will'.

Roy and I were grateful to God that we had such a good relationship so that when he became ill with cancer there was no remorse, no guilt, just sadness but with an inner peace, knowing that God would work through the particular circumstances we found ourselves in. We didn't have to fight but simply trust in the God who said he would never fail us or forsake us.

During the time Roy had cancer our faith was tested many times and in many ways. However, this was also the time when we realised that applying God's principles in the everyday trials pays dividends when the bigger problems raise their heads. In fact six months before Roy became ill, God had challenged me with a verse from Job: 'Though he slay me, yet will I trust in him' (13:15, AV). Job I tried to fathom what God was saying, though it didn't take a lot of intelligence, just bottle! I sensed God saying, 'You've trusted me through the good times – now are you prepared to trust me in the tough times, and can I trust you with the tough times?'

I knew ultimately there was only one answer to that question – yes. After all, who else could I trust? Hadn't I tried and failed through many years before I finally put my trust in Jesus? I believe God was preparing me for the moment when Roy came home to tell me he had lung cancer. I remembered that God said '*When* you go through the fiery trials ahead' not '*if*' (1 Peter 4:12, New Living Translation). God is looking to see how we handle the trials of life and we have much to learn from every one of them.

Many, many times I would hear Roy say, 'Well, Lord – this isn't the way I would have chosen it, but if this is the way you want it – that's OK with me.' Roy's prayers were always devoid of spiritual jargon and his relationship with Jesus was simple and straightforward, as it was with people.

People ask me how I am and I can say 'fine' with honesty. I can echo Roy's prayer. It's not the way I would have chosen it, but it has happened this way and I am glad to make the most of the circumstances in which I now find myself. I have nothing at all to grumble about and I certainly don't want to be classed as a victim of my circumstances! Far from it. I am grateful for all God has taught me through these past years. I have nothing but gratitude for the life I've lived. A visit to my daughter who lives in Peru taught me that!

We have food – we have water – we have heat – we have shelter – we have money – we have medical attention. All those commodities which we so often take for granted are lacking in the shanty towns of Lima as they are in many of the developing countries. One thing the Bible teaches is available to all: our faith in God through Christ Jesus.

I am grateful to God every day that I am fit and well to keep 'running the race'. I had a choice. I could either have withdrawn from the world and grieved behind the closed curtains of my home or I could rise to the challenge and pursue the opportunities which God seemed to be presenting to me. After all, I don't know how much longer my life will be and if I waste opportunities I will live with regret as well as grief! How much better to look outward towards others rather than looking inward and expecting others to meet our needs. If we live with that expectation we will always be disappointed.

It is not always easy to discern God's will as new opportunities present themselves and I know sometimes I get it wrong, but I tend to go for a gut feeling of peace. If I get it wrong, well, God knows that my heart's desire is to be obedient to him and to 'run with patience the particular race that is set before [me]' (Hebrews 12:1–2, The Living Bible).

If doubt ever creeps into my mind or if God seems a million miles away, I think back to the day he so radically changed my life. Nothing could ever persuade me to go back to the way I was before Jesus changed me, so I trust God in the silence and rest my case.

2

Surprising Grace

J. I. Packer

Whose decision?

Just as I was about to start writing this essay, I learned that the book it is for would be called *The Best Decision I Ever Made*. (The provisional title was different.) That discovery floored me at first, for this title, taken in its natural sense, has nothing to do with what I am going to write about. The best decision *I* ever made was to try to persuade Kit to marry me (she did, thank God); and I shall go down to the grave insisting that my assigned topic, namely my becoming a Christian and the difference it made, was not a matter of *my* decision, but of the Father, the Son and the Holy Spirit bringing home to me *their* decision regarding me. So it began, so it continues, and so it will be to all eternity. (All who know God know this, deep down, though they do not always find it easy to say, and sometimes get tangled up trying.)

Speaking for myself (which, after all, is what I am supposed to be doing), I have to say categorically that I do not appreciate decision-language in Christian evangelism and nurture, and do not myself use it. Why not? Because it naturally implies that one is choosing between alternatives any of which one is free to reject; and in processes of genuine spiritual significance, starting with conversion, whether as a child, an adolescent or an adult, I do not believe that to be the case. Scripture and experience (all the experience that in my fifty-five years as a Christian I have ever had or heard of, anyhow) unite to tell me that in true conversion one is only free to bow to God, come to Christ, leave the old life behind, and accept that a new era has opened. God has made the decision, and now the Trinity has invaded (or have invaded – either is correct). There is an inevitability about the responsive acknowledgement you know you must make. To appeal for decision in the way some do, as if you could and would do God a favour by embracing the option he has just laid before you, is to lose touch with the way things are, and to risk generating an unreal sense of the situation that is likely later to boomerang when the decision-makers sense the manipulation and the hollowness of what they were told to do as response to what they heard. The same is true throughout our Christian lives. We make our own decisions about material and temporal things, and devotional instructors are constantly appealing to us to do this or that. But the really decisive decisions, those that affect the growth of our relationship with God, are decisions that we are made to feel are God's rather than ours, decisions which we accept rather than make. Certainly, that is my story, and I am sticking to it, as the following pages will I think show.

On the road

I am desired to say something about my own conversion. I present it as the sovereignty story that, both at the time and since, I felt it to be.

Father was a clerk on the Great Western Railway, running the General Office of the Gloucester division. Mother had been a junior school teacher, and had come under high Anglican influence while at college. I was the older of two children. Home had a faint Christian flavour, for we went to church once each Sunday, but we had no family religion, we did not say grace at meals, and we did not talk about the Christian faith (apart from the one time Father flew at me for saying that sometimes suicide might make sense). I suppose it was Mother who taught me to say my three simple prayers at bedtime, but doing so was just routine, like cleaning one's teeth. My idea of God as a benevolent potentate was more pagan than Christian. I did not go to Sunday school. I was growing up a lower-middle-class snob.

The sovereignty story starts here. At age seven I suffered a head injury that left me with a hole in my skull. That meant that when World War 2 came, the Forces had no use for me, and I was able to go up to Oxford in 1944.

At age fifteen I played chess with the son of a Unitarian minister, who between games tried to interest me in pacifism, Esperanto and Unitarian beliefs. Unitarianism denies that Jesus is God while praising to the skies the neighbour-love side of his ethic. I saw this as raising a dilemma: if you disbelieve something so basic to the New Testament as Jesus's deity, should you not write it all off? But if you think Jesus's moral teaching has divine authority, should you not ascribe the same authority to more of what the New Testament says? Unitarianism struck me as arbitrary, held together by willpower and fashion rather than by any sort of logic, and that set me wondering what truth there really might be in Christianity. To find out, I borrowed from the public library; I chewed C. S. Lewis, that most chewable apologist, whose *Screwtape Letters* I met as required reading for general studies at my state school (imagine!); soon I was sure that historic Christianity made sense, and was substantially true, and I was ready to debate our sixth-form atheist, a brilliant German Jewish refugee, on the matter. Meantime, I became a conscientious church attender and an active member of the youth group, even going to camp with them (a near-heroic act, for I have always found camping repulsive). I had become priggishly religious.

At age seventeen a school-friend who had preceded me to university wrote to say he had been converted and could see that I had not got faith. I had no idea what he was on about, and told him so. At that time his mother, who had an uncanny clairvoyant gift, told me I would end up a clergyman. I thought this ridiculous, since I knew I had no message for, and frankly took little interest in, those around me. But I was not worried; complacency triumphed again.

At age eighteen I went up to Oxford. My friend had begged me that when I got there I would link up with the Christian Union who, he said, with what in retrospect appears as sweet humility, would be able to explain about faith better than he could. I have always wanted reality and been caustic (in my thoughts, and sometimes in my words too) about people who seemed, one way or another, to settle for less, so I did not hesitate to follow his advice. In the second half of the first Christian Union-sponsored evangelistic sermon I heard, much suddenly became clear. I realised I was being shown that for all my orthodoxy I was still outside the Christian life because I had kept the Lord Jesus at a distance, and he himself was now coming close and putting me under pressure to change that. A shock to my system? Yes. While we sang 'Just as I am' I did what my heart told me to do (it was, as you see, a very ordinary conversion), and then for four years I enjoyed fellowshipping with, and being discipled by and learning ways of ministry from the Christian Union membership. Some immaturity was there, but also much reality, and my whole involvement, which grew into a larger, lasting bond with the worldwide Inter-Varsity movement (Universities and Colleges Christian Fellowship in Britain, International Fellowship of Evangelical Students globally), always felt like a further decision that God made for me, and that I could not but accept.

In my day, as since, the Inter-Varsity movement has distinguished itself by standing for the truth and trustworthiness of the entire Bible, the need for all doctrines to be based on the direct teachings of the written Word, and the prime importance of studying and meditating on the Bible as a discipline of the Christian life. I should therefore record that while I did not bring such convictions to Oxford with me (my belief being just a general assent to the creed), I found from the day of my conversion that the New Testament simply glowed (no other word fits) as I read it. Six weeks after, having taken into a Christian Union meeting for Bible exposition my shallowly arrogant assumption that no intelligent person in 1944 could seriously treat everything in the Bible as true (cognitive dissonance? looking back, I think so), I came out sure that Scripture is God's own Word, given and applied by the Holy Spirit, and divinely true throughout. I still recall my feeling of mild surprise at myself and at my new sense of certainty. What had come to me, as I now know, and come rather vividly, as it sometimes does, was what Calvin calls the inner, secret witness of the Holy Spirit to the divinity of the Scriptures, a sense that the God who spoke and speaks the text now speaks in and through the text in an applicatory and commanding way – an awareness which, according to Calvin, every Christian enjoys. At that time I had not read a word of Calvin, nor ever heard of the witness of the Spirit, but that evening I knew it first-hand, as by God's grace I still do. God had decided to convince me, and I was convinced.

So with the later impact on me of Reformed and Puritan theology, with my subsequent work as an adult educator and author, with our move to Western Canada in 1979, and with my fifty-year quest for evangelical revival and in particular Anglican renewal both sides of the Atlantic: God, it has seemed, had made the decisions, and my part was simply to go along with what he had laid out for me. If my life has been a *passacaglia*, the prevenience of grace has been its ground bass. 'From him and through him and to him are all things. To him be the glory for ever. Amen' (Romans 11:36 NRSV). God does not change, so I expect that life will go on like this for as long as it lasts (that, too,

I know, is something God has already decided), and then I shall continue to adore my decision-making God in the bliss beyond.

The difference grace has made

Self-analysis is not easy, and I do not claim to be good at it. What you read here is the best I can do. My account of myself cannot, in the nature of the case, be definitive; in this world we never know ourselves fully, nor do we ever see all that God's grace has done for us. But clearly it is hoped that I shall say something about how being a Christian has done me good, so I must try.

As a believer, I know, because the Bible and the Holy Spirit in my conscience unite to tell me, that I am a sinner whose inner twistedness is unsearchable, and who every day falls short of God's standard at every point. But I also know that Jesus Christ my Lord with his Father foreknew me, loved me, gave himself on the cross for me at his Father's will, and now stands by me to keep me going; and that through regeneration and co-resurrection with him I, the personal self that currently lives through my body, am really though invisibly and mysteriously united to him by the Holy Spirit in a vital relationship that grows here and now and will keep on growing for ever, unimpeded by the disembodiment of death, the re-embodiment of resurrection, and the demolishing and remaking of the universe all around me when Jesus returns. I know that I am forbidden to be prideful, or fearful, or self-pitying, or despairing, or bitter, just as I am forbidden to be dishonest and malicious and self-centred, or to womanise or become a miser or a drunk or a sycophant (flatterer, as the Bible puts it; creeper, to use the slang of my youth). And I know that without Christ some if not all of these things would be a greater part of my track record than they are at present. Love and care for others do not come naturally to me; they have always been an effort. No doubt I am in many respects, perhaps in some of those mentioned, worse than I know. All I can say for sure is that I would certainly be worse than I am were it not for the grace of Christ.

I can put it this way. The biblical books I prize most are those that I, like others, have found richest theologically – the Gospels, Romans, Ephesians, Hebrews, 1 John, and the Psalms. But the books that grab me as C. S. Lewis and John Donne grab me – that is, because the writer deep down seems to be my sort of person on my sort of wavelength – are Ecclesiastes and Ezekiel – which tells you a lot about the natural Packer straightaway.

Ecclesiastes, 'the pundit' as his title may fitly be rendered, is not a pessimist, as is often thought, but a realist with a strong sense of the tragic quality of life 'under the sun', where so much effort and so many good intentions simply get wasted, and so many hopes of significant and satisfying living are dashed. Ecclesiastes is pained at this, yet not bitter, for he knows that the God in whose providence grandiose plans fizzle gives to some, at least, present joy in simple things – work, meals, marriage – and will reward all the godly faithful in due course. Ezekiel is a priest, a patriot, and a loner, a rigid logician without much human warmth but with a vivid, Bosch-like sense of how people cheapen themselves and become brutish and nasty as they follow the lead of their mindless self-centredness. He is repelled by the ugliness of their ungodliness, and feels acutely the pain of being one whom they proudly pooh-pooh. Ecclesiastes is not a cynic, only a spokesman for clear-eyed realism, and Ezekiel is not a cynic, but rather a prophet of restoration; both of them, however, would surely have slumped into cynicism, for sheer self-protection against further hurt (the root of most cynicism in this world), had it not been for their faith in God.

Now, in terms of temperament I find myself identifying with both men at a very deep level. I describe myself publicly as an Ecclesiastes man; I could just as truly call myself an Ezekiel man. For I too am by nature a loner and an outsider, and my pre-Christian experience of life as I recall it was of feeling hurt and disgusted. That, so far as I can see, had nothing to do with what my parents or peers or pedagogues were like, only with how I processed things. Mother warned Kit when we were courting that I would be a grumpy old man by the time I was forty, and I certainly would have been had not Christ had his way with me. The temptation to react to life by sliding into cynicism still grins through the window; I do not expect it ever to leave me. But as a Christian I have wallowed in the joys of which Ecclesiastes spoke, and in Ezekiel's confidence that where sin now abounds grace will finally overflow and superabound, and thus I have been turned into a kind of person that by nature I never could have been.

When you know that you live in the love of a sovereign God, fear and hopelessness and the suspicion that nothing is worthwhile, all of which in my case were reinforced by great shyness and awkwardness, give way to cheerful peace and unquenchable hope as your inner condition. Paul generalises about this, clearly speaking from his own experience of it.

> Since we are justified by faith, we have peace with God through our Lord Jesus Christ, through whom we have obtained access to this grace in which we stand; and we boast in our hope of sharing the glory of God. And not only that, but we also boast in our sufferings, knowing that suffering produces endurance, and endurance produces character, and character produces hope, and hope does not disappoint us, because God's love has been poured into our hearts through the Holy Spirit that has been given to us. (Romans 5:1–5, NRSV)

> Who will separate us from the love of Christ? Will hardship, or distress, or persecution, or famine, or nakedness, or peril, or sword? ... No, in all these things we are more than conquerors through him who loved us. For I am convinced that neither death, nor life, nor angels, nor rulers, nor things present, nor things to come ... nor anything else in all creation, will be able to separate us from the love of God in Christ Jesus our Lord. (Romans 8:35–9, NRSV)

Following along far behind, I resonate with all of that, and thank God constantly that it is so.

Surprises

Now in my seventies, with over half a century of Christian living behind me, I can testify that God in grace has given me a life of fulfilment that were I not a Christian I would never have had. To start with, there has been fulfilment for the mind. Christianity, which here means the teaching of Christ and his apostles and the entire Bible, plus the central stream of faith over nearly 2,000 years, has given me cogent and satisfying answers to all the great nagging questions: Where did I come from? What am I here for? What is really worth doing? What should I believe? What may I hope for? These answers turn out, as in this century men like Chesterton, Lewis and Schaeffer have shown so well, to make perfect sense of literally everything in this space–time order of reality in a way that no alternative view of life ever has done or, I venture to think, ever will do. To see this, and to keep verifying the insight against the endless flow of non-cogent alternatives, stabilises and satisfies the mind in a decisive way.

Secular thinkers, modernist and post-modernist, liberal and Marxist, think of Christianity as a facile optimism that cannot cope with today's knowledge about the nature and history of the world, nor account for the actual quality of human experience, with its tensions, tribalisms, barbarisms, brutalities, madnesses, miseries, emptiness and despair. But precisely the reverse is true. Christians – who recognise that the basic dynamics of human life are, first, sin – original sin, as Augustine called it – corrupting all natural instincts and desires by giving them some form of egocentric twist and, second, God's grace in Christ redeeming and restoring while a subserving providence restrains the total chaos that sin would otherwise bring about – can account for all the realities of disordered human existence, which the other views cannot do. And biblical theism, with its grasp of the transcendence and immanence of the triune God, proves constantly able to take on board all the knowledge of historical events, physical processes and operations of the psyche, that modern research yields, without being undermined or overthrown. What I have said may surprise some, but factual enquiry will show it to be so.

Then there has been the fulfilment of doing whole-heartedly a series of things that when put to it I found I could do. In this regard the God who made me, and changed me, and knows me better than I know myself, has frequently surprised me with his decisions for me. That I should, after all, become a preacher and pastor, a man with a message from God; that I should find I can help people learn, and so become a college teacher of theology as well as being a church teacher of the Bible; that I should also become a pastoral author, producing resource books on faith and life for God's people; and that Kit and I should emigrate when we were both over fifty, and enjoy in Vancouver the best twenty years of our lives, while I taught at Regent College, gave the world a book a year, and did what I could for the Anglican Church of Canada: these events formed a series of surprises, moves not dreamed of till God made me aware of what he had decided for me. Left to myself, without God's amazing grace shaping my life, I guess I would have drifted into mediocrity as a schoolteacher, with my heart not deeply committed to what I was doing and my cynicism deepening every year. But as it is the sense of fulfilment, of doing what I was made for and redeemed for and am constantly being enabled for, has been strong throughout, and remains so as I write now.

Words we sang at our wedding may well close this confession, or striptease, or progress report, or whatever you like to call it.

> How good is the God we adore,
>   Our faithful, unchangeable friend!
> His love is as great as his power,
>   And knows neither measure nor end.

'Tis Jesus, the First and the Last,
    Whose Spirit will guide us safe home.
We'll praise him for all that is past,
    And trust him for all that's to come.

3

A Night on the Streets in Brazil

Sarah de Carvalho

It is 10 o'clock at night, Thursday 19 November 1998. The air is still very warm, from the sweltering summer sun of the day. My legs ache from walking. My head feels dizzy from the stench of the *tiner* – strong paint solvent – that the kids sniff compulsively off dirty rags. This is just one night out on the streets with some of the members of our street team. We've been on the move since 7.30 p.m.

'*Eu vou passar* (I'll go through),' says Paul bravely. A young missionary from England, his Portuguese is excellent after only eight months. He grabs hold of the iron gate and hoists himself up and through the only narrow opening available. The thick wire mesh that covers the iron bars has been ripped open just wide enough for a slim human being to squeeze through.

Dora and I strain our eyes into the sea of darkness, trying to make out if any of them are there. A few months earlier this filthy place was 'home' to many a street gang. The padlocked gate leads the way into a long yard, the size of a tennis court, which runs along the side of a large derelict warehouse situated near the centre of the city. The thick concrete wall surrounding it is too high to jump over, making the gate the only access point.

With what little light there is from a streetlamp on the other side of the wall, one can make out piles and piles of mouldy litter scattered everywhere. Suddenly Dora and I see the shadow of a figure moving out of the darkness from the far corner of the warehouse.

'*Oi, quem esta ai* (Hi, who is it)?' cries out Dora into the night. There is no reply. Whoever it is starts to walk slowly towards us.

'*E nos de Crianca Feliz* (It's us from "Happy Child"),' I shout. Still no reply.

'Quick, Paul,' calls out Dora nervously. 'I think he's got a knife, get back quickly through the gate.'

Like lightning, Paul leaps back through the small opening, cutting his finger on the thick wire mesh and bruising his side.

'Ouch!' cries out Paul in pain.

'Who is it? We're from *Crianca Feliz*,' persists Dora, her dark Brazilian eyes glistening anxiously.

Finally we can make out who it is. Edson. Nineteen years old, he's been living on the streets from the age of five. I remember him from when I first arrived in Brazil in 1991. Fair-skinned and gaunt, he was small for his age. He's often said that he could never leave the streets. 'I'll live here until I die here,' Edson had once told Dora. She'd stepped up her prayers for him ever since.

'Where are the others?' I ask. A pretty black teenage girl, half dressed, has also emerged from the darkness closely behind Edson.

'They have moved 200 yards down the road,' he answers, rolling his words from the effects of the drugs. 'I'm just taking a shower in the warehouse and then I'll be joining them later.'

Some shower, I think to myself. We set off to find the gang . . .

Why is Christianity important to me? It isn't a religion. It is a person.
Jesus Christ. He came and met me where I was. He accepted me.

Successful but empty.

Rich but poor.

In a relationship but in sin.

Travelled but restless.

Smiling on the outside but crying on the inside.

He told me he loved me. He led me to the foot of the cross. And once there he didn't let go of my hand. The weight of sins that had blinded and bound me were taken away. Then he led me into the transforming presence of a living God. What used to make sense suddenly didn't and what didn't make sense suddenly did. I was given the assurance that there is a destiny. I realised all at once that I wasn't only flesh, blood and bones, but had a spirit, a soul that was starved. It was as though I'd only been living half alive those previous twenty-seven years.

'The Spirit and the bride say, "Come!" And let him who hears say, "Come!" Whoever is thirsty, let him come; and whoever wishes, let him take the free gift of the water of life' (Revelation 22:17). The love he filled me with was greater than life. It was such that I knew I couldn't keep it for myself. A light had been turned on in the depths of my being.

A compassion awoke . . .

'Sarah,' exclaims Dora, 'It's Rodrigo!'

We've finally reached them. Their camp of cardboard boxes and black dustbin liners is precariously erected alongside a railway line and the main city road. There is a patch of grass between the road and their camp where four of them are kicking a football around. Brazilians can't live without their football whatever their circumstances! The three of us are quickly surrounded by sixteen watchful faces of all different colours and sizes.

My heart sinks as I slowly register Rodrigo. I haven't seen him for a long time. He's changed. Oh, boy, how he's changed! A front tooth has gone. His head is covered in bald patches where his lovely thick brown hair has fallen out in clumps. His hazel-brown eyes have a wild, even mad look to them. He has grown in height but, my goodness, he's so thin. Too little food, too much abuse. How much can a human body take? He is sniffing solvent on a rag even as he looks at me, his eyes narrowing, his head turning on one side, as though he were a hawk eyeing his prey.

'*Tia* (Aunt),' he manages to say. 'H-o-w o-l-d is y-o-u-r son?'

My goodness, he can remember. He can remember! Rodrigo had come to the farm when he was fourteen years old. Three years earlier. Up to then, he'd lived on the streets for as long as he could remember. The only person he'd liked on the farm, however, was my elder son Lucas, who was a toddler of two years old at the time. With everyone else on the farm he'd fought, both physically and verbally. With Lucas he'd always turned into marshmallow! It was fascinating to watch.

However, the lure of the streets had been too much for Rodrigo. He'd missed the drugs. He'd missed the sex with his own kind. He'd missed the false 'freedom' of doing what he wanted when he wanted. He'd missed the stealing. He hadn't wanted to go to school or to work. Rodrigo, in other words, did not want to change.

He had had many other chances, but never took them. Now he was too old to come into our programme. Happy Child is structured to take in children and teenagers, both boys and girls, between six and fourteen years old. Once in the programme they can stay, if need be, for as long as it takes to rebuild both their lives and that of their family, if they have one.

'You had the chance to live with Sarah and her family at the farm and you didn't stay?' asks Aldair, a handsome boy of sixteen standing next to Rodrigo. Aldair sounds incredulous. 'I can't believe it. You really are crazy, Rodrigo. I never had a chance like that in my life!'

Aldair turns and whispers loudly in my ear, 'He's gone mad, you know. Too many drugs.' A lump comes into my throat as I look at Rodrigo.

Then Paul says excitedly, 'Good news! I've just heard from

one of the girls in the gang that Tereza has gone to the *Casa Nova* (Happy Child's day care centre). She's now off the streets!'

Street work is not easy. Sometimes there will be weeks of seeing the fruits of our labour and other times there will be weeks of seeing very little. Paul had told me of this young girl, Tereza, aged eleven years, whom he'd met living with these older boys a week earlier. He'd been very concerned for her safety. Now we are all happy to hear this news.

Paul goes off to play with the four footballers on the tiny patch of grass. Dora had sat down on the kerb with the others. I go to join her, followed closely by Aldair and a very drugged Rodrigo. I look at my watch. It is 10.40 p.m.

'I w-a-n-t to g-o with you, *Tia*, to the f-a-r-m,' says Rodrigo. His words all roll into each other.

'You can't go to the farm any more, Rodrigo,' answers Dora kindly. 'You'll have to go to *Dom Bosco*. They have a restoration house especially for older teenagers.'

'I'll go there tomorrow if you give me the address,' chirps in Aldair.

Dora goes to ask Paul for his pen.

'I don't like the other boys at *Dom Bosco*,' states Rodrigo sulkily.

'There is nothing wrong with the ones I know who live there,' I tell him.

At 11 p.m. we start walking back to the main bus station. We have to get buses home and most of them stop running after midnight. It is very tough leaving the kids behind knowing that they'll sleep on the hard pavement. It always is. Tougher because this older lot have all been on the streets for years, and most have had many chances to get off. 'Their problem', you might say? But somehow there is always hope.

'I can't bear it,' mourns Dora sadly as we walk on. 'Seeing those young men living like they do. It's worse knowing that they've all had chances to change.'

'Be strong, Dora,' I try, feeling low myself. 'Think of all those

28

hundreds of boys and girls that we *have* taken off the streets into Happy Child over the last five years!'

'Yes, you're right,' responds Dora, rallying.

It's the story of the lost sheep, I think to myself, *you can rescue and pen up hundreds into safety but when there is still one out there bleating away on the edge of a mountain cliff, wounded and hungry, you leave the rest and go after it. Don't you?*

Three hours earlier we had found five-year-old Taniane and her brother Diogo and older sister Tania. Their mother, Angela, also lives on the streets. Angela was drunk. Very drunk. Her husband, their father, had been murdered a week earlier . . .

Why is Christianity important to me? 'Delight yourself in the Lord and he will give you the desires of your heart. Commit your way to the Lord; trust in him and he will do this: He will make your righteousness shine like the dawn, the justice of your cause like the noonday sun' (Psalm 37:4–6).

For me this meant letting go of my career in film promotion and television production, at the age of twenty-nine. It meant letting go of my fears that if I went single I'd never get married. Letting go of my church in London, Holy Trinity Brompton. Letting go of my country, my language, my culture, my home, my friends, my social life. But above all it meant letting go of my Dad, Mum and two sisters, Maria and Vanessa.

I'd said to him, 'Here I am, use me!' It wasn't easy. It still often isn't. But he had a plan for my life. I had to trust him. Nevertheless, every great test has prepared me for every great victory. And the victories keep me going. Because the victories are tremendous. God prepares his chosen, refines us, so that Jesus will shine. The greater the work in us, the greater the work through us. The deeper the work in us, the deeper the work through us.

What was my choice? I heard that children were living on the streets, in the gutters because they had nowhere else to go. Old before they are young. Dead before they are dead. When I heard that in Brazil they were killing them, what was my choice? I had no talents nor training to work with children or teenagers. I couldn't speak Portuguese. But he called me. He asked me to go. And I thought, 'How can I say no, if Jesus can reach and save just one of these street children through my life. How can I say no?'

A candle loses nothing lighting another candle. However, the trials come:

- The homesickness;
- Missing a long afternoon chat at my sister's;
- Missing dressing up and going out for dinner with childhood friends;
- Not bringing up my children the way I was brought up;
- The smaller challenges of a cross-cultural marriage;
- Not being able to visit my Mum for tea with the kids;
- Not going to my home church whenever I want to;
- Speaking another language in another culture;
- Then there are the challenges of founding and co-running a large ministry;
- Standing firm in the vision through the trials;
- The spiritual warfare;
- Living by faith for finances;
- Keeping unity in a large team of over fifty workers;
- Seeing a street boy come off the street into the day care centre, then on to the night shelter and finally the farm – two years later he leaves the farm rehabilitated, full of the Holy Spirit, working and studying – then six months later he throws everything away and joins a gang in the worst favela (shanty town) selling drugs;
- The perseverance, faith and price paid in intercession every time we open a new house for the children – forming the 'right' team, finding the right structure, and trusting in God to provide the finances and to sustain us through the ups and downs until the work is producing fruit;
- Trying to move forward – believing in what we can't see with our physical eyes but can with our spiritual eyes through prayer – God's plans, God's timing.

However difficult these are, I know deep in my heart that through each trial and sacrifice God uses them to refine me. He makes trouble a door of hope. And the victories do come. And the desires of my heart:

- A husband with the same heart and vision for God;
- Three beautiful children;
- A cheque in the post with a note saying, 'This is for a romantic dinner for you and Joao!'
- A new church;
- The memory of an outreach to an island off southern Chile, with dolphins, meadows of wild flowers, incredible birds, white-capped mountains and three good friends;
- The ability to learn a new language;
- The love and understanding of a new culture;
- Sunshine every day!
- An anonymous couple paying the rent for our apartment when we felt it was time as a family to live separately from the ministry after nearly four years on the farm;
- A phone call from a great friend in England when I was feeling blue;
- A cheque from a deacon at our church in Belo Horizonte a week before Lucas was born – they had been told by God in prayer to give us money towards doctor and hospital fees. (We had no money and had told no one of our need);
- Mum and Dad here on holiday;
- My sons Lucas and Daniel praying with a faith that makes me cry;
- Sharing Christmas dinner with over fifty children and teenagers who would otherwise be on the streets;
- Seeing the joy on Juarez's face when he went back to live with his Dad after years on the streets;
- Welbert, ex-gang leader, ex-prisoner, six years on the streets, giving his powerful testimony of how Jesus changed his life to around two thousand young people, after two years on our farm.

> Hundreds of people that night responded to his call and gave
> their lives to Jesus;

- Being sung to on my birthday by all those beautiful boys on the
  farm – 'blessings upon blessings';
- Seeing Ze Geraldo working in a popular Pizza Restaurant in
  Belo Horizonte with a smile that could break a thousand hearts
  – the victory of a young boy transformed;
- Seeing Alfanazio, aged thirteen, on his knees with tears pouring
  down his cheeks in church, oblivious to those around him,
  thanking Jesus for taking him off the streets and giving him a
  new beginning;
- Witnessing the power of prayer as our rehabilitation house for
  street girls starts to fill up and God's hand starts to move
  through their precious lives. Receiving the news that all eleven
  girls are attending school. We'd been considering closing it three
  months earlier;
- Celebrating the birthdays of Ana Luisa, Polliana, Pamela and
  Arli with a party for over seventy people (both children and
  workers), which was only their dream when they were once all
  living on the filthy streets;
- A pastor from Ethiopia telling us that God had told him that
  Joao and I were tired and needed a break – he paid for four
  nights at a country club including meals;
- A deeper relationship with God as my heavenly Father . . .

'Angela', I had said, 'Your children cannot stay on the streets
with you any longer. You are in no fit state to look after them.'

Diogo, nine years old, and Taniane, five years old, were both
jumping on to Paul's back, giggling. Their tiny limbs were filthy,
their dark thick hair matted and they wore no shoes. Tania,
eleven years old, was off talking to a gaggle of drunken women
and men sleeping rough on top of cardboard boxes next to us.
These really are the dark hidden places in cities that few see, I thought
to myself once again, *it's another world.*

Angela was forty-four years old. She looked sixty. Small and emaciated, her brown face showed the haggard signs of alcohol abuse. One of her eyes had a cataract. She had nine children from three husbands, the latest of whom had been knifed in a bar across the street. She was desperate. She wept, as she thought of him. They'd both lived on the streets together. She told us that God had forgotten her.

'He hasn't, Angela, that is why we are here,' I answered her with conviction.

'Angela,' said Dora, 'Let your children come to *Casa Nova* tomorrow. They can take a shower, have new clothes, eat a good meal. They need to get off the streets. They need to go to school. It's too dangerous for them here. Tania could be raped.'

Angela agreed. She could hardly stand. Paul arranged to pick up Tania, Diogo and Taniane the next morning to take them into the day care centre. When we left, Diogo was crying. Angela grasped the money he'd begged for in her hand. He wanted her to buy him a kebab for his dinner, she was thinking of her next drink . . .

Why is Christianity important to me? Jesus said that what is impossible with men is possible with God (see Matthew 19:26). I have seen that as I step out in faith and do what is possible for me, God does the impossible. This is when my faith and trust in him has grown. He is so near. He is so faithful.

At the end of The Street Children of Brazil *I wrote that we were currently halfway towards our attempt to purchase the farm from the Lagoinha Baptist Church in Belo Horizonte, who had allowed us to use it during the early years of our ministry. However, we still owed the staggering sum of US$140,000, which we had agreed in faith to pay off in three instalments in 1996: US$50,000 in May, US$40,000 in August and the final US$40,000 in November.*

Now I think back to the events which led up to God's miraculous provision of this money. In February, we received another donation from the same family in Singapore whose generosity had enabled us to embark on the acquisition of the farm. This covered the May instalment; but by the due date for the second payment we only had US$10,000 in our bank account, money that some local churches in Belo Horizonte had donated. The Lagoinha church began to put pressure on us because they had a huge building programme of their own and bills to pay. In the middle of all this, Joao left for a three-week trip to Mozambique, Africa!

'What shall I do?' I asked Joao in desperation. 'You can't leave me here alone with all this pressure.'

'Sarah, don't worry, God is in control,' was Joao's reply.

The whole ministry got on their knees.

Two days after Joao's departure, Marcia, his assistant, phoned me, to tell me of a strange dream she had had.

'All the workers and the children were marching around the farm buildings, praying and singing, just like Joshua and the city of Jericho,' said Marcia. 'I believe this is linked to the buying of the farm.'

Suddenly I knew without a doubt that God was indeed in this. 'So let's do it!' I said to Marcia. 'We've got nothing to lose. The Bible says that the ways of God are not our ways. And he got his people to do some pretty surprising things in the Old Testament!'

That very night we all gathered in front of the main white farmhouse, and I explained about Marcia's dream. Opening the Bible at the book of Joshua, chapter six, someone read the account of the fall of Jericho's walls all those thousands of years ago. Well, we didn't want the farm buildings to fall down, that was for sure! But just maybe something powerful was going to be broken in the spiritual realms. 'I will give you the keys of the kingdom of heaven; whatever you bind on earth will be bound in heaven, and whatever you loose on earth will be loosed in heaven' (Matthew 16:19).

We decided to march around the farm buildings seven times, praying and praising God between each march, and claiming the farm in the name of Jesus for his work with these children. What a bunch of amateurs we were! Our singing was flat and our marching out of step! Most of the boys thought it all extremely funny! At the end of the exercise, we said goodnight to one another.

'Oh, well,' I said to God as I returned alone down the hill to our *little family house, 'make the best of what we did, if you can!'*

The night that followed was the most exhausting I ever remember. I had nightmares and my bedroom felt full of oppression. Next day we called a meeting.

'Whatever we did last night, however ridiculous it seemed to our human perception, has stirred up things in the spiritual realms,' I explained. We asked the Holy Spirit to direct our time of worship and intercession.

No one will ever forget the time which followed. The Holy Spirit came upon us, the atmosphere was permeated by an invisible presence that settled like warm dew. All at once people started to pray out loud with words and an authority that could come from no other source but God himself. This was spiritual warfare, and Jesus was right there with us. He broke the plans Satan had to stop the will of God taking place on that farm in the future. The farm is a place he uses to help bring children off the streets and into his arms. It is a place where they can be children once again; go to school; play sport; work on the land; train for a future. Suddenly a sense of peace filled the room, a sign for us all that in the spiritual realm, a victory had been won, the issue was settled.

After the meeting we felt God wanted us to repeat the march on two further occasions. The first took place early the next morning, and we decided to fast also. Many of the boys and some of the workers looked far from convinced, but this time we were better organised. Ingrid our worship leader led us, followed by some of the boys playing their recorders. There were about forty of us in all. We prayed before setting off, and God gave me a prophecy which I spoke out in faith.

'I believe God will release some money after this march.'

'Amen,' said some.

We set off, worshipping and praying as we went. And then it happened – as we approached the farmhouse after our seventh circuit, the telephone could be heard ringing.

'Sarah, it's for you!'

I listened to the caller in awe . . . Someone had placed US$23,000 in our account. What a time of celebration!

'Let's march again!' cried the boys, now fully animated.

'I think we should have a time of thanks and praise,' said little Juarez with his gorgeous smile. Just to see the faces of those precious boys! They had been part of a miracle. And before we'd finished celebrating, two further amounts were deposited in our account that day, bringing in the exact amount we needed for the second instalment.

We completed the third march a week later. It was the most joyful and enthusiastic march imaginable! By October, a whole month before we were due to pay our third and final instalment, Happy Child had already received the amount needed. The farm was ours!

We have such a faithful God. I am learning that it is best just to obey even if it doesn't make a whole lot of sense at the time. His ways really are not our ways.

We left Angela and her three children and headed for that derelict warehouse via the central train station where many usually spent the night. On the way we met Renato and Wesley walking in the opposite direction. Renato is the brother of Washington and Juarez, both of whom have spent over two years on our farm and are now back living with their father. Washington used to pray for his little brother every day, when he lived with us. But Renato continues to choose life on the streets.

'Renato,' cried out Dora, 'Where have you been? I've missed you!'

Renato giggled and sniffed the dirty rag in his hand. Wesley had died his hair blond, and it was sticking up in all directions. He was tiny and wore a T-shirt and shorts that were about four sizes too big for him. I grabbed hold of little Wesley and gave him a hug. He didn't resist.

'We've got to go, Tia,' insisted Renato.

'No, no, no, you don't!' exclaimed Dora. 'Come on, let's sit down together on the pavement. I've got something to show you.'

Wesley was now jumping all over Paul. Dora opened her

handbag and took out a little closed box. This grabbed the curiosity of the two boys who quickly knelt down beside her. I noticed a series of parked cars nearby. Two taxi drivers watched us, perplexed. That part of the city was quiet for that time of night.

'Let me open it, let me open it!' shouted Renato enthusiastically, his large brown eyes showing his excitement. He'd quickly forgotten about his urgency to move on.

Inside the little box were hundreds of tiny coloured cards. Each card had a Bible verse written on it. The two boys took it in turn to choose a card, eyes closed. Dora read the verses out one after the other. They loved it. Seven minutes later, the game had lost its momentum.

'Renato, your brothers are missing you,' I tried. 'When are you going to join them? Are you going to spend the rest of your life living like this? Go to *Casa Nova* tomorrow.'

Renato, ran off laughing, closely followed by little Wesley.

At the central train station we saw Marcio. He'd been living at *Casa Emaus* (the night shelter) for three months and had gone back to live with his mother.

'What are you doing here?' Paul asked, concerned.

'I was missing the drugs,' admitted Marcio. Thirteen years old, he wore a permanent cheeky grin, highlighted by his large white sticking-out teeth.

'Marcio, don't throw away all that you have been given. Go to *Casa Nova* tomorrow morning,' I said firmly. 'I'm going to call there first thing to make sure you're there. If you're not, I'm going to be very upset.'

'No, I'll go there, Sarah. I'll go there,' insisted Marcio.

He was doing drugs with a small group of street kids and teenagers. They were leaning against the side of the main building close to the front entrance to the station. As we were talking to them, a teenage girl of about eighteen years old began to cry. I asked her what was wrong.

'They've taken away my baby and put her into the FEBEM

(government home for children),' she answered, tears streaming down her brown cheeks. She sniffed some more of the solvent.

'Why are you on the streets? Go and live with your mother and they'll give you back your baby.'

'I can't. My mother's house is too small.'

'You could go to Youth With A Mission's house for teenage girls,' I suggested. I felt the pain of what it must be like to have your baby taken from you, whoever you are and whatever your circumstances.

'I don't want to,' she said.

I looked around at some of the older teenage boys in the gang and got a clearer picture of her dilemma.

'If you love your baby, then you must do everything to get her back and bring her up yourself,' I said to her, gently.

I suddenly noticed a bundle lying on the pavement at the corner of the main building under a covered area. We went over to investigate. Paul knelt down and lifted up the filthy blanket.

'He's not well,' said a woman with no teeth, close by. She was drinking.

'It's Daniel,' said Paul.

Daniel wore only a pair of shorts. His little brown body trembled.

'I think he's got a fever,' said Paul.

'How old is he?' I asked, my mother's heart breaking.

'He's about nine or ten years old,' answered Paul. Daniel was exhausted and didn't want to be woken up. He was lying on some dirty cardboard. I stood up and called over to Marcio.

'Marcio,' I shouted, 'can you take Daniel with you tomorrow morning when you go to the *Casa Nova*? He's sick.'

'I will,' promised Marcio.

We walked on to our last stop of the night, that derelict warehouse.

Why is Christianity important to me? Jesus said:

*For I was hungry and you gave me something to eat, I was thirsty
and you gave me something to drink, I was a stranger and you
invited me in, I needed clothes and you clothed me, I was sick and
you looked after me. I was in prison and you came to visit me . . .
I tell you the truth, whatever you did for one of the least of these
brothers of mine, you did for me. (Matthew 25:35–40)*

This was just one night on the streets with the street team. They go
out every morning and two nights a week. The outcome of that
particular night was encouraging. Marcio and Daniel are off the streets
and living in Casa Emaus, our night shelter for boys. And I have
recently seen little Daniel well, nicely dressed with shoes and socks on
his feet at a birthday party at the girls' house. Moments like this
make the trials seem trivial.

Angela and her three children – Tania, Diogo and Taniane – were
taken by Paul into the Casa Nova the next day. They attended the
house for a week, then a relative collected them all and took them to
live in their home.

Joao had a meeting with the local government the following day.
They asked if we would be interested in opening a 24-hour drop-in
centre for the older teenager living on the streets. The government
respect our Christian faith and recognise that over the last five years
we have taken more children off the streets than any other organisation
they help support. As a ministry we continue to pray for God's
confirmation about this centre.

What are my own personal and spiritual hopes for the future? In
Belo Horizonte, fewer children on the streets, and the continuing
development of our work here in Brazil. In Mozambique, Africa, the
establishment of a Happy Child mission base. There are over 300,000
orphans as a result of the brutal civil war that lasted for seventeen
years. I have faith that we can bring to hundreds of them a new hope,
a new beginning and a new future when God says to us, 'IT'S TIME!'

4

The Discovery of My Life

Michael Green

I was born in 1930, in the Depression. Perhaps that is why I had no brothers or sisters: finances did not allow it. Or could it be due to my father's reaction to being one of twelve children?

My parents were poor in money but rich in love, generosity and self-sacrifice. My mother was an Australian who had given up her native land and come to Britain to marry a Welshman she had met only once on a visit, but who pursued her with his letters. My father was a country clergyman, looking after two tiny rural parishes, the only incumbency he ever held. He faithfully served those parishes for more than thirty years.

We lived in one of those massive old country rectories which immediately set a barrier between the parish priest and most of his parishioners. It was the big house, and to live in it inevitably isolated you from the villagers. So there was quite a solitary aspect to my youth. I went to the village school just across the road, but most of my spare time was spent behind the great gates which closed off the rectory drive, making my own entertainment in the near three acres of garden. Situated as we were seven miles from the nearest town, I began to develop a deep love for nature and the countryside, a love which has never left me. Birds, fish, wild animals, butterflies – I was fascinated by them all.

When I was seven years old a big change occurred. My uncle ran a preparatory school, and he offered my father to take me as a pupil for the princely sum of five pounds a term. This seemed too good an opportunity to miss, because my parents could never have afforded the full fees. Looking back I am most grateful for my uncle's generosity. But at the time I felt I was being wrenched hundreds of miles away from my home into an environment which I did not understand and where I was left very much to sink or swim.

I loved the holidays. When that battered old black suitcase was loaded with me on to the train home, I was elated. I knew a royal welcome awaited me. As my father's ancient Austin seven, which had met me at the station, puttered into our drive, my mother would run out with almost unbearable joy to hug me and bring me into the house, where a great treat was to have pork sausages for the welcoming first evening meal. One thing was clear to me about boarding-school. It did lead me to appreciate my home all the more.

While I was at home I regularly went to church on Sundays. It seemed the least I could do to help my father who, as was very obvious to me at an early age, was battling against the decline of organised religion that has marked the twentieth century in the West. He was struggling to keep the church an effective force in the village. So I backed him up, and so did my mother. It would have been unthinkable to do anything else in those days, and in any case I wanted to help. That is why I gave as much assistance in the house as I could. That is why I hand-mowed the interminable lawns in the garden. Others might think it was a privilege to live in a big house, but even my young eyes could see that with no finances to keep it up, and no help to speak of in house or garden, my parents needed any small contribution I could make. I even sang in the rudimentary choir which the church boasted, though I croak like a raven. At school we had formal prayers every day, and formed a long crocodile to a particularly dreary church on Sunday where my headmaster uncle was a sidesman.

I was lazy but bright, and in addition to my five canings I remember getting the odd prize for school work, including Scripture. I was a lawbreaker by instinct, and was generally involved in the illegal activities that went on – smoking, beating other boys up, climbing out at night and so forth. A disturbingly violent streak was beginning to become evident, and my language grew increasingly foul – a habit I could not stop even at home, where it was a distinct embarrassment!

Enough of those early days. I realised with a shock in my penultimate year at the school that unless I started working, the future of my education was very much in doubt. So I applied myself, lazy though I was by temperament and experience, and in due course got a scholarship to Clifton College, Bristol, which the school authorities generously increased because we were not able to afford even the reduced fees. And so in 1945 I began what I suppose has proved to be the most decisive five years of my life.

I had not really enjoyed my preparatory school, but I loved Clifton. When I first went there, the school was still in the evacuation quarters it had taken over during the war. Bristol was a dangerous target area for German bombs, and in any case the army soon requisitioned the school buildings. So my first two terms were spent in what had been, in peacetime, a terrace of hotels by the seashore in Bude, Cornwall. It was wonderful. The freedom, the wild midnight excursions, the rock-climbing and abseiling, the opportunities for entomology, shooting, cricket, fencing and all my other distractions! And on top of all that, the privilege of a good education which offered a wide variety of specialisations. I have fond memories of that first term at school when six of us junior boys were herded into what had been a single hotel bedroom, but now housed six bunk beds, roughly lashed together, leaving practically no floor space. That was where we lived. We quickly formed a close bonding, and before long were making gunpowder which we delighted to explode in all the most inappropriate situations. Little monsters that we were, we constructed blowpipes which shot darts dipped in the formic acid which we distilled! Naturally when these touched the skin of our human targets, they tended to scratch, and the inflammation grew.

Such was the scene when a boy in my house invited me to come to a private – almost secret – meeting. It took place in the cricket pavilion on a Sunday afternoon, now that the school had returned to Bristol. It was to do with Christianity, and it amazed me, because it immediately showed me that Christianity was very different from what I had assumed hitherto. Some forty boys were listening attentively to the Professor of Surgery at Bristol University, who also, I discovered, edited the *British Medical Journal*. He was talking about Jesus Christ. And to my astonishment he spoke with a quiet conviction that Jesus was alive! Now I knew a good deal about this Jesus. He had formed a background warmth to my growing up. I had read the Gospels and had even won a prize on them. But nobody had ever suggested to me that Jesus was still alive, and that he could make a real difference to the lives of twentieth-century people. Yet clearly here was a highly intelligent scientist who not only believed it and lived in the light of it, but thought it so important that he was willing to give up his valuable time on a day off to instruct a bunch of schoolboys on the topic! It set me thinking. If this professor and the group into which I had unwittingly tumbled was correct, then they had made the most important discovery of all time. If they were wrong, I need not trouble myself further with Christianity. It would prove to be merely a matter of following the ideals and teaching of a revered but dead teacher, and that need not make any serious impact on my life.

I was resolved to find out whether or not they were right! So I decided to do two things. I would regularly attend the meeting of these enthusiastic friends of Jesus, and see what I made of their teaching. And I would watch the members during the week, and see if this profession that Jesus was alive made any difference to the way they behaved. I could see this was an intensely important issue. Was Jesus really alive, risen and relevant? Or was he just one more great teacher who had come to a sticky end? This question, and its implications, was the most important issue one could possibly consider. It was quite literally the key to the meaning of existence. I was determined not to be taken for a ride. I needed to examine it carefully for myself.

So I watched the members of this meeting for some eight or nine months, during which time I regularly attended their weekly gathering. It was led by Richard Gorrie, the head boy of the school, who was a brilliant academic and a distinguished athlete. One summer Sunday he gave a talk on God's guidance. By that time I was clear that I could no longer resist the claim that Jesus was alive. The difference he made to the boys who professed to believe it was too blatant. From an investigator I had turned into a seeker. I was now convinced that this stuff was true. I realised it was all to do with Jesus. But to me he was still the stained-glass-window Jesus, the Stranger of Galilee encased in the dusty books of the New Testament. And I was fed up with religion; I was hungry for reality.

So I went up to Richard Gorrie at the end of his talk and asked him how God guides us. It was not a very flattering question, come to think of it, since he had already delivered an excellent twenty-minute dissertation on the subject! He looked at me with a wisdom beyond his (nearly) eighteen years, and invited me to come to the upstairs storey of the cricket pavilion. And there he led me to a living faith.

I cannot recall all that happened that Sunday afternoon. But the main outlines are burnt into my memory. I remember the cricket bats and pads, the spikes in the boots and the divots of turf on the heavily scored floor. I remember him gently pointing out to me how I had affronted God by my way of life. And I did not argue. He had, only the term before, been obliged to give me a richly deserved punishment for illegal entry into his house at the school! I knew my life was a mess. I did not need to have it rubbed in.

But then he showed me something obvious enough, but I had never seen it before. He showed me that Jesus Christ had done all that was necessary to bring me back to God. On the cross he had taken responsibility for all the dark side of my life. I already believed in my vague way that Christ had died for the sins of the world. After all, it came across in almost every service. But it had never meant anything much. That afternoon I saw that he had died for *me* personally, bearing responsibility for *my* failures and deliberate bad things. It was the evil in me, among others, which had held him to that cruel cross. He had done it willingly, in his great love. I seem to recall that Richard gave me a graphic illustration of the difference Calvary had made. He used the prophecy in Isaiah 53, and illustrated the phrase 'All we like sheep have gone astray' by placing a black object between his left hand and the light. That represented the responsibility for my misdeeds resting upon me, cutting me off from the light and the warmth of God's holy love. 'We have turned every one to his own way'; I could not quarrel with that. I knew it was true. 'And the Lord has laid on him the iniquity of us all', continued my friend, transferring the dark load to his other hand, which stood for Christ dying upon the cross. Of course this released the left hand, which represented me. No longer need there be a 'cloud of unknowing' to separate me from God. I saw for the first time in my life that Christ had carried my burden of evil, he had taken personal responsibility for all that was wrong in me. The whole lot was poured on his sinless head, so I could go free. And the love of such a God broke me down.

But that was not all. My second shock that afternoon was occasioned by my friend's gentle question whether I believed that Jesus Christ had risen from the grave. I had long been able to say the creed without it affecting me in any way. My searchings over the previous months had convinced me that Jesus was indeed alive, and I had no difficulty in telling Richard so. He then faced me with a crunch question. 'What are you going to do about him, then?' I began dimly to see that I was faced by a massive choice. I could either disengage from this Christ who had loved me and given himself for me, or else I could yield my whole life, future and career to him. There was no middle way. I was on the horns of a dilemma. I had to choose.

That led to my third discovery that memorable June afternoon. I must have told him that I had no idea how to react to the enormity of what God in Christ had done for me. So he took me to a verse in the Bible which has led its millions to a personal commitment. It was Revelation 3:20, where the risen and ascended Christ says these wonderful words to a lukewarm church, lukewarm because they had kept him excluded from their church and personal lives: 'Behold, I stand at the door and knock; if any one hears my voice and opens the door, I will come in to him and eat with him, and he with me' (RSV).

Though there was much I did not understand, the heart of the matter was now sufficiently plain. The Jesus who had dealt with the barrier which seemed to make God so far away, the Jesus who had smashed the power of the Last Enemy by the great victory of Easter Day – this Jesus, Son of the living God, was alive. He was willing and able to enter my life by means of his Holy Spirit. Of course, Christ himself had returned to heaven at the ascension, but I do not recall that this posed any problem to me. He was apparently willing, indeed enthusiastic to place his unseen Spirit in my life, and start living in me. What an exciting, if daunting, prospect! It was undreamed-of generosity for God to act like that.

However, it would be very demanding. It would require the cleaning up of the mess in life. I could not do that: I had tried. I vaguely realised that Christ could do it, but I had to be willing for the revolution to start inside me. My sins were comfortable. Like ivy on a tree they had been intertwined with my life for many years. It would be hard to break free from them. And it would mean that Jesus, not I, was henceforth to be Number One in my life, my behaviour, my decisions, my ambitions, my relationships. Was I prepared for such a costly takeover? And then, of course, I would not be able to keep quiet about this overwhelming discovery. I would have to be willing to 'let my light shine' as the Gospels put it, and once I knew a bit more, I would need to be Christ's vocal ambassador as well. How much I understood of all this that Sunday afternoon I do not know. But I know I counted the cost of discipleship as best I could.

Richard helped me to see what needed to be done by showing me a postcard of Holman Hunt's famous painting, *The Light of the World.* It was inspired by Revelation 3:20, and shows Jesus Christ, clad in dazzling white and with a blood-red cloak, standing outside the door of a dark and desolate cottage. In his hand he holds a lantern – is he not the Light of the World? Clearly he looks for access, and then the light will illuminate all the house and shine out of the windows. But equally clearly he will not enter until he is invited by the tenant. The door is choked by ivy: it has never been opened. Yet patiently Christ stands knocking, with the nail marks in his hand. He is waiting to be invited in. He is offering to come in and stay for ever. The imagery was lucid and compelling.

That afternoon I gladly and deliberately accepted Christ's offer. I did so with tears of gratitude (yes, tears from a reserved male in mid-teens, tears that hit the dust on the floor, and bounced). I blurted out my response to him in a prayer, and I am grateful that I was encouraged to begin my active discipleship with an audible prayer. Many churchpeople spend fifty years and more in church and seem unable to pray out loud. It has no particular merit, of course, apart from concentrating your thoughts and enabling others to share in your petitions. But that in itself is not unimportant.

When I had recovered from what, for me, was a very emotional act of will, my friend started to give me some immediate aftercare. He told me how to meet the initial doubts that were sure to come from the Father of Lies. To begin with I would have no experience to depend on, but I had the promise of the Christ who could not lie: 'If any one opens the door I will come in.' Well, that 'anyone' covered me. I had 'opened the door' of my will. So he *had* come in – because he had pledged to do so. I could rely on his promise. He could not break his word. That was a great help to me later that day; I relied on his promise and I found it beginning to become true in experience. I suppose I was learning one of the basic lessons of faith: believing the promises of God and resting my weight on them.

Richard then tried to get me introduced to a rudimentary devotional life. He suggested that I should forthwith get up when the first bell went in the house I belonged to, at 7.10 a.m. There was a second rising bell at 7.25 and all boys had to be on parade for 'call-over' at 7.30 (on pain of a caning for three absences!). Those of us with some bravado made a point of not stirring until the second bell went. Indeed, I used never even to hear the first bell. When I told this to Richard he was somewhat nonplussed, but responded very wisely, 'Ask the Lord to wake you up at the first bell, and then get up and spend a bit of time with your Bible and in prayer before the day gets under way.' I was prepared to give that a try. And to my amazement I found that I did wake up the next morning at 7.10, and continued to do so every morning during the rest of my time at school. Those fifteen minutes or so before call-over, in the privacy of a loo, proved invaluable for getting me into the habit of devotional Bible reading and prayer. I remember I started reading Romans. I had never been able to make head or tail of the Epistles before my conversion, but now they began to speak to my new experience of life with Christ.

Before I left that afternoon Richard encouraged me to talk to the Lord as I went along the road back to my house. I did not need to shut my eyes or kneel down. I had encountered 'the Friend who sticks closer than a brother' and it would become the most natural thing in the world to speak to him, and listen to him, at any time and on any topic. In this way I began to learn how to 'abide' in Christ and live my life with growing awareness of his companionship.

There were two particular ways in which Richard Gorrie was of further help to me. In the first place he invited me to a Christian houseparty for boys in the holidays. I had heard of this, and had already turned down an invitation because I very much enjoyed my holidays at home. But now I saw that it would be a great way to develop my Christian life, and I enthusiastically accepted. That houseparty became an important part of my adolescent and young adult life. I learnt a relevant and attractive pattern of Christian discipleship among boys my own age, specifically related to life in a boarding-school. And when I became an undergraduate and began to help in the leadership of this houseparty, I found I was given a marvellous training. Indeed in three areas I have never met anything superior: how to give an attractive talk, how to lead an inductive Bible study and how to engage in basic pastoral work. All this lay in the future, but I know that the friendships, worship, fun and teaching of this holiday houseparty and term-time school meeting were an enormous help to me in the formative period of my active Christian discipleship.

The other great help Richard afforded me was this. He made himself available about once a fortnight to answer the questions and objections I had about the Christian life. I used to make a note of them as they cropped up, and saved them up to talk over with him. He would answer them to my satisfaction, and then choose a short passage of the New Testament to read with me and show me how to draw thoughts from it for my own life. This personal one-to-one care is sadly missing in many parts of the Christian world today, and it is immensely valuable. I might well have foundered without it.

You may wonder what differences began to emerge? They were fairly visible because I had been quite a high-profile troublemaker! One was my language. I found that the habits of swearing and obscenity, which had held me in such a tight grip, disappeared almost overnight. I learnt to pray with the psalmist, 'Set a watch, O Lord, before my mouth; keep the door of my lips', and to my amazement within a few weeks every trace of it had gone. The other thing was my violent temper. I was a passable boxer, and I used violence on people outside the ring too, when my Welsh temper flared up. But once I had entrusted my life to Christ and asked him to work on this problem I found I did not even want to hit them!

I do not think that these two failings were particularly important in themselves, but they mattered to me, and I had been quite unable to get rid of them. The power of the risen Christ made short work of both. It was an enormous encouragement to me, as you can well imagine. I think God often gives graphic and immediate answers to prayer in the early days of our Christian lives to help us get started in trusting him. Later on it seems to be much slower and more gradual.

The remaining years at school saw solid growth in my Christian development. I began to try to please Christ in every aspect of my life, probably becoming for a while unnecessarily narrow in what I allowed myself – but maybe that was a good failing. I found I was becoming very keen to share the joy of Christian faith with others who seemed as blind to it as I had been. Naturally, I was not competent to help them to faith myself yet, and that would have been politically unacceptable within the closely bound network of an English public school. But I was able to invite them to the same houseparty which had so helped me, and had the joy of seeing several boys becoming firmly committed Christians as a result. I guess that is where the seeds of evangelism were sown in my heart. They have persisted and indeed grown ever since.

I also discovered the joy of close Christian fellowship with my peers. A number of us who were school prefects were also committed Christians, and we used to meet regularly to pray for each other and for the school. No doubt we were somewhat precocious, but all the same it gave me a taste of close Christian fellowship. And this has seemed to me to be one of the most lovely aspects of Christianity as I have, in subsequent decades, moved widely around the world. The Trinitarian God, who not only invented fellowship but *is* fellowship, has so arranged things that it is in fellowship that we find our greatest fulfilment, and supremely in fellowship with those who have Christ in common.

I had two somewhat painful experiences during my school and student days which taught me an important lesson. In my last year at the school I was very surprisingly picked as the opening bowler in the school cricket eleven. This was a high honour in those days, and we all greatly looked forward to the culmination of the season, a three-day match against Tonbridge School at Lords. Well, I was dropped before the Lords match. And it hurt. But it taught me not to make an idol of sport, as I was tending to do. Then after five terms at Oxford we classicists had an examination which constituted the first half of our degree. It consisted of thirteen papers, and you needed six alphas in order to get a first class degree. I worked hard, and hoped I might make it. In the event I got five alphas, and six b++ marks. I later learnt that they had discussed my case at length – and I was given a second. That taught me not to make an idol of academic success, as I was tending to do.

If those were examples of God teaching me through comparative failure, one particular incident from my student days stands out as God guiding me very clearly towards the life-work for which he had designed me and in which I would be most fulfilled. At the start of my penultimate year at Oxford I would have expected to go into either the Foreign Office or maybe academia after graduation. I often prayed that God would guide me between the two. But one day I heard a sermon saying that we should not give God a choice of options but rather ask what he wanted us to do. So I began to pray like that, and gradually the conviction began to take shape that I should offer for the Christian ministry. That was most certainly not part of my plan! I loved being a Christian but had no desire whatever to be a professional cleric. One night the local curate dropped in for a coffee, and I remember asking him, 'Teddy, why should I be a wretched parson? I'm just not going to do it!'

Rather than arguing, he sat down, clutched his coffee and roared with laughter. 'Of course you are, Green,' he said. 'It's perfectly obvious.'

That was actually just the treatment I needed. So that night I knelt by my bed and prayed with great sincerity. I told God I was willing to be ordained if I must, but that I did not want to make a mistake which would mess up my life and the lives of thousands with whom I would come in contact. And so I asked him to give me a sign. I do not advocate that procedure, by the way! But I did ask for a sign that night.

Next morning the president of the university Christian Union called in, most unexpectedly, and asked if I would be willing to become president the following year. This was a great surprise to me, because I had been far from assiduous at their meetings. So I went to see my tutor and asked him if I was likely to get a first in the final part of my degree. He told me that I would get a second standing on my head, but would not get a first. Had he told me that I was a likely candidate, I would have turned down the Christian Union. As it was, I felt free to take it on. And what a good decision that proved to be. It meant the experience of leadership among several hundred of my fellow students at a particularly important time when Michael Ramsey was about to come and lead a mission to the university. And it meant that I met my future wife on the executive committee! But at the end of it all, when I sat my finals, I turned out not merely to have got a first but one of the best ones in the year. It taught me a powerful lesson about God's guidance. And I began to realise that when you start following the path of obedience to God you are not the loser.

That year of leadership in the Christian scene in the university was invaluable for me. It confirmed my call to ordination. It launched me on the path of public speaking, thoughtful leadership, and extensive reading as a Christian. Followed, as it was, by the practical knockabout of two years in the army on national service, with the opportunities for evangelism that offered, it prepared the way for a research degree at Cambridge while training for ordination. And that calling is clearly what the good Lord designed me for. I have been extremely happy and fulfilled in it. If I had my time again I would take precisely the same route. It has meant teaching in theological colleges and universities in England and abroad. It has meant travel in the cause of the gospel over much of the world. It has meant many missions in universities, towns, cities and villages in England and overseas. It has meant seeing many men and women turn to Christ and many enter ordained or missionary service alongside the majority who have allowed their faith to shine through so-called secular careers. It has meant a good deal of writing, radio and television work in the cause of the gospel. It has opened the way for the great privilege of spending twelve years as a pastor in a very lively church. And it has led to the joy of seeing four Christian children all launched on useful careers.

And if from one perspective it all began in the mysterious election of God before I was born, from another it sprang from the decision made back in those mid-teen years to entrust my life to Jesus Christ. It was without question the best decision I ever made.

5

Rediscovering Our Roots

Michele Guinness

Sometimes, when I'm sitting in church, it occurs to me, if Jesus walked in now, would he know what this was? And when he broke bread and blessed the wine, as the Jews do every Friday evening, did he really say, 'From now on I want you to have a special liturgical service in a holy building, say some set prayers, walk unenthusiastically out to the front, line up in an orderly row, stick one palm out beneath the other, chew on a manhandled morsel of dry bread or paper-tasting wafer, wet your lips with wine, then wander back to your seat looking suitably awed by the piety of the occasion'? The other, nonconformist method of passing lots of tiny, individual glasses down the rows seems equally incongruous. As far as I'm aware, all he said was, 'When you do eat and drink together and say the traditional Jewish blessings, remember me.'

As a Jew, raised with traditions which have changed very little in essence from that time, I tend to wonder, as he must, how the church got from there to here. How did it become so dreary, so lacking in colour, warmth, community and celebration, so far removed from anything I vaguely recognise?

When my children were small they arrived home from school one day chanting:

> Roses are red,
> violets are bluish,
> if it wasn't for Christmas
> we'd all have been Jewish.

Nice attempt to defuse anti-Semitism early, but playground twaddle all the same. Without Christmas I would have been Jewish, my children would have been Jewish, while their Gentile friends would have been little pagans. But because of Christmas, or at least the incarnation, Christians are reborn into a Jewish world – children of faith through Abraham, a wild olive grafted into the original tree, with a Jewish Messiah, Jewish apostles and a Jewish book as their inspiration. Surely that must make the church a little bit Jewish?

That can come as a shock. I'm used to the idea. I confront my heritage every time I look in the mirror. Had I been able to afford a 'plastic nose job' and gone blond without a perpetual battle against dark roots, I would have done so in the early days of my conversion. I so badly wanted to blend, chameleon-like, into my new surroundings, to be a pale and interesting Anglo-Saxon if not a classical English rose – anything but a swarthy vaguely continental-looking Semite.

But we grow up, hopefully, out of the insecurities of youth. Gradually, I began to realise that my inheritance might have relevance, not simply for me and mine, but for a church which appeared to have lost any sense of its origins, and being rootless, was often weak, bland or insipid.

I always assumed that the church had simply drifted from its moorings the more Gentile it became, but on my first trip to Israel, awaited with anticipation until my children were old enough to appreciate the sites, I discovered to my amazement that those ties had been deliberately hacked and severed.

Mystifyingly, many people seem to assume I was either born in Israel or pop backwards and forwards at whim. Nothing could be further from the truth. I don't identify easily with contemporary Israeli culture. I'm as British as they come, a Geordie from Gateshead of immigrant peasant stock – though it doesn't sound as exotic. I was raised in the little mining town of Felling on Tyneside, daughter of the local GP whose penniless Latvian parents fled the pogroms in Eastern Europe, *Fiddler on the Roof* style, and found a safe haven on the freezing, windblown, north-east English coast.

But on that first visit, Caperneum, the apostle Peter's home in Galilee, reminded me of Felling as it was in my childhood – a hugger-mugger of tiny, back-to-back, higgledy-piggledy, stone-terraced dwellings with certain basic communal facilities. No one could yell at the spouse or the kids, or have digestive problems, without entertaining the entire neighbourhood.

Some of the first Christians met in Caperneum, out of doors in a shared courtyard in the summer, packed into a home like pilchards in the winter, men, women and children intimately participating in every aspect of each others' lives, their faith fully integrated into the daily grind.

From Caperneum we were taken thirty miles down the road to the ruins of the sophisticated Roman city of Skiapolis, with its fine architecture, beautiful houses, amphitheatre, temples, roads, shops, and oh joy, proper plumbing. The church that grew here, some fifty years later, met, not in a home, but in a more central location, and was more formal, more hierarchical, more cerebral, more sophisticated. And it is this Greco-Roman, rather than the Jewish model which we have inherited today.

The demise of the Jewish church was a slow process, the final and deliberate death blow dealt by the Emperor Constantine in the fourth century when he ostensibly converted to Christianity and made it the official religion of the Roman Empire, which, ultimately, did the church no favours. For that temporary release from persecution there was a heavy price to pay. Institutionalising a living entity effectively stifles the life out of it.

Constantine couldn't stand the renegade, rebellious Jews, challenging both his and the church's authority. The Council of Nicea in 325 AD, responsible for drawing up the Nicene Creed, the faith basis of many churches, also issued an edict claiming that Jewish practice was superstitious jiggery-pokery and any Christian keeping a Jewish festival would be excommunicated. The calendar was altered so that the crucifixion and resurrection would be moved away from the Passover and celebrated at the pagan Easter feast, despite the Levitical law commanding Jews to keep the Passover even after the Messiah had come. Tabernacles or Booths, rich in messianic symbolism, was replaced with a pagan harvest festival. The Sabbath was also moved to the first day of the week to coincide with the pagan Sun Day, and Saturday declared a preparatory fast day so that Jewish Christians would be unable to celebrate appropriately and end up torn between the two. Effectively, they and their traditions, the heritage of Jesus himself, were banished from the church. Constantine's mother, who had a penchant for vast Roman-style edifices, built magnificent but impersonal cathedrals throughout the Holy Land on all the intimate early church sites.

The established Roman Church grew more powerful and corrupt over the years, stamping out any deviation in its faithful which might weaken its control. Even the lively, indigenous Celtic Church in Britain, which had managed to preserve a more Jewish spirituality, integrated in the nitty-gritty of home, family and community, was subdued.

I knew none of this as I struggled to make sense of the church and where I fitted. I only knew it seemed cold, austere and rather pompous compared to the synagogue and the festivals celebrated in our home. Tempted by a group of friends at school I popped in from time to time on a Sunday evening on my way to the Jewish youth club. The club was a perfect cover. It meant my parents didn't need to know I was going to church. The very idea would have appalled them. A night club was more acceptable, with the right escort, of course – a nice Jewish boy with good material prospects.

Dressed in my best ritzy-glitzy disco gear, skirt halfway up to my neck, eyes made up like a panda, and a red Mary Quant PVC mack and matching hat which squeaked in the sombre ecclesiastical silence every time I moved, I wasn't exactly the usual kind of punter at Anglican evensong. In fact, this refined, awfully English congregation had never seen anything quite like it. But their unbelieving stares didn't manage to put me off. Something drew me back, despite the quasi-Arctic conditions in the building, undefeated by the mediaeval heating system, and my inability to find my way around the Anglican prayerbook or kneel at the same time as everyone else. It certainly wasn't the post-service coffee, served in green, pitted china cups in a room behind the church with beige walls and peeling, maroon skirting-boards.

A schoolfriend persuaded me to read the New Testament. 'Well, you've read the Old,' she said. Little did she know. I had read Genesis and Exodus in ancient Hebrew, tortuously translating it word by painful word at compulsory Jewish classes, three nights a week for one hour and on Sunday mornings for two. Six years of translation practice began to feel like a forty-year journey through the wilderness. The children of Israel still hadn't found their way out when I did, my parents putting an end to my misery, afraid that too much religious tuition might interfere with my schoolwork. My biblical knowledge, not to mention my Hebrew, was still rudimentary. When I stood up in the synagogue to join in the prayers I could read the text fluently. I just hadn't a clue what I was saying.

I started reading John's Gospel at night under the bedclothes by torchlight, so as not to disturb my younger sister, the Bible on one side of me, *Lady Chatterley's Lover* on the other. They were equally forbidden books. Gradually, the New Testament won. Precocious sixteen-year-old that I was, there was nothing in *Lady Chatterley's Lover* I didn't know. John's Gospel, on the other hand, was a revelation. I was even unaware that Jesus was Jewish – not like I was, at any rate. In representations I had seen he was always blond, blue-eyed, fair-skinned and Western. Pitifully pale and thin, he floated around in a long, white gossamer nightie, perfectly pedicured, his feet barely touching the ground, with an expression of inimitable empathy carved on to his plaster-of-paris face. The gospel, flesh-and-blood Jesus was swarthy and strong, robust and sweaty. He was a man who couldn't stand hypocrisy and cant and I liked that, for I couldn't bear it when orthodox relatives donned phylacteries and read morning prayer for all to see, before they went for a bacon breakfast or were uncivil to their neighbours. Jesus could look inside the human soul and see the secrets hidden there, those you wouldn't admit to yourself, let alone another. And somehow, I didn't mind.

At a school trip to the York Mystery Plays, as I watched the cross being hoisted in the air with Jesus hanging on it, I understood, with a comprehension beyond normal rational functioning, that Jesus was the fulfilment, not the negation of my Jewish background. There was no Old and New Testament. In the Old the New was hidden, in the New, the Old made sense. The key which finally unlocked the door was Jesus's words to the disciple Philip, 'He who has seen me has seen the Father'. The Father had chosen us as a people. He was faithful, merciful, but distant. Jesus on the other hand was utterly accessible, a tangible reflection of the sacrificial love of God, the Messiah. It all made sense.

But not to my parents. 'Christian' had all sorts of negative connotations – crusades, pogroms, forcible baptisms, concentration camps, Hitler. This was a betrayal, a denial of all they had brought me up to be. And, to get to the heart of the matter, it meant that they could kiss goodbye to any hope I might marry a nice Jewish boy. Which one would have me now?

Ostracised from the Jewish circle, it was imperative I find security and acceptance within my new community. But I was a misfit. This was the 'we don't dance', 'we don't party', 'we don't go to the theatre', 'we don't wear make-up' or let-the-wicked-swinging-sixties-seduce-us era. There were so many don'ts this seemed a faith with more rules and regulations than the Mishnah, the Jewish law. Sometimes I conformed, mainly I rebelled, and managed to attract a reputation for being 'fast' – though in fact there was little opportunity as I terrified any Christian boy who came within a pew's width. Fortunately the wind of charismatic renewal began to blow some of the stuffiness away, and I met a man determined and forceful enough to take on his match.

It wasn't until the children were born that I really began to question the brand of Christian spirituality I had inherited. A 'quiet time', half an hour of Bible study and prayer first thing in the morning was essential, apparently, for the day to go well. With a baby and toddler demanding every minute of my waking attention, I now realised that had been the unappreciated luxury of a bachelor girl. How could I pray when the children followed me everywhere, even to the toilet, banging on the door and screaming? Every book on prayer I read had been written by men. I was doomed, for what seemed forever, to a spiritually vegetative state.

The whole idea of 'families who pray together, stay together' compounded my guilt. How were we to do that? Should I say to the children, 'Stop playing, we're going to pray' or 'Turn off the television, we're going to read the Bible together'? Nothing could be more guaranteed to turn them off God for life.

I began to reflect on my upbringing, on the Sabbath Friday evenings, when my gregarious, socialising parents chose not to go out, my mother lit the Sabbath candles, my father read the familiar prayers and we drank sticky Palwen red wine, ate the sweet, plaited chollah bread and a traditional Sabbath meal of cold fried fish; on the great festivals like Passover, New Year and Tabernacles celebrated around my grandmother's table, laden with familiar mouth-watering goodies, the cloth bleached to dazzling cardboard stiffness, the polished silver reflecting a dozen distorted mirror images of our faces, and the wine glowing like liquid rubies in the goblets. We sang, we prayed, we joked, we gossiped, we laughed, my grandfather fell asleep while leading the service until my grandmother snapped at him in aggravation. It was all one seamless whole. There was no, 'fold your hands, close your eyes and bow your heads, we're going to pray', no division of what was spiritual and what wasn't. It seemed to me, as I remembered it, that Jews don't attempt to pass on belief, but rather an indescribable feel for a Jewish way life, a climate in which faith can blossom. While Christians, who know rationally that belief cannot be enforced, try and do so anyway, without instilling any feel for a Christian way of life.

I wanted my children to grow up with their spiritual life as real as their physical existence, where prayer was as natural as breathing and when they eventually left home, the Christian faith associated with all the best, not the boring, moments of childhood. So we introduced a Sabbath eve, one night when we were together as an extended family, inviting adopted grannies and aunties from our church family, since our real family lived so far away. I lit the candles welcoming Sabbath rest, and prayed for my children as my mother had, laying my hand on their heads and asking God to make them grow up as faithful as Abraham, Isaac and Jacob, the patriarchs, or as fruitful as Sarah, Rebecca, Leah and Rachel, the great mothers of Israel, and in his time to send them good spouses who would care for them. We shared a cup of wine, symbol of relaxation and rejoicing, and a plaited loaf representing the work of human hands, remembering how Jesus had given his flesh and blood for us.

Joel, at three, entered into the occasion from the first. He prayed for those who had no work, and those who had no bread, in fact he prayed halfway round the world, and after a while I began to wonder if we were ever going to eat. In time the children accompanied the singing with a medley of makeshift musical instruments, combs wrapped in greaseproof paper, knives on glasses, spoons banged together. We gave them small weekend gifts – usually chocolate.

Today they are adults and whenever they're at home Friday night, or whatever night we decide to set aside, is still a treasured cacophony of singing, prayer, laughter, favourite food and fellowship.

It was a while before I realised that if Jewish-style celebration could offer a basis for family worship, it might reinvigorate the church. By that time Peter had been ordained, a further test for my long-suffering parents who were only just coming to terms with my marrying a Gentile. Mother's Sabbath prayers were not quite answered as she had expected. I told her she should have prayed harder. 'Who knows,' she said wryly to my father, when the initial shock had worn off, 'I might yet be mother-in-law to the Archbishop of Canterbury.' It's my fervent Sabbath prayer she never is.

Tentatively, we offered our congregation in Coventry a full Passover meal and service, not a demonstration. We felt it had to be experienced with the senses, rather than understood with the mind, and expected a dozen or so intrepid volunteers. Two hundred people signed up. It became a logistic nightmare. But they loved it, so much so, that in every church we've been in, it becomes a ritual we can't shake off, not even for a year.

Passover is the great freedom festival when the Jews celebrate their miraculous deliverance from slavery in Egypt. It's a wonderful parable of all Jesus did for us at the cross and he used the symbolism at the Last Supper as a kind of audio-visual aid, so that on every subsequent year the disciples would make the obvious connections. Children participate fully, in asking set questions, in recounting the story of God's faithfulness to his people, in chewing tear-jerking herbs like horseradish in memory of the bitterness suffered by their ancestors, in singing familiar hymns and hunting for the *Aficomen*, a piece of matzah which represents the Passover lamb and is hidden away, then suddenly rediscovered, or resurrected. This is the piece of unleavened bread Jesus shared with his disciples immediately after the meal, at the moment when he said, 'This is my body broken for you.'

People tell us that once experienced, they can't imagine Easter without it. It conveys the bittersweet emotion of the Last Supper, that final celebration which Jesus looked forward to sharing with his followers, probably with a heavy heart, before he faced his destiny. A traditional communion service on Maundy Thursday just isn't the same.

If Christians are going to become a more celebratory people, returning to their roots to retrieve the dynamism and colour lost so long ago, I don't think they need to adopt the Jewish festivals, familiar to me, but not to them. It may primarily mean celebrating the Christian festivals better. Harvest and Pentecost are often damp squibs. Christmas and Easter, pagan in their origins, have been swallowed up in secularism. It's time for the church to reclaim them by rejecting a Hellenistic mindset for a Jesus-like world view. That means several basic principles are at stake involving our perceptions of God, Jesus and who we are as God's people.

First and foremost, our God is too small. Celebration grows out of an awareness of our place in his eternal scheme of things. It gives our lives meaning and takes away the sting of their brevity. But unlike the Jews, Christians have very little sense of their history. When we lived in Coventry a friend described crossing the city the morning after the blitz to visit her sister in hospital. All the landmarks had gone and she couldn't find her way around. Without the past, the present is a disjointed, meaningless fragment of time. So we say to God, 'What's your plan for my life?' rather than, 'What's your eternal overall plan and where do I fit into it?' If we only see our tiny bit of the story we have a very limited, distorted view of the author. Suffering, victory, pain and joy can get out of proportion. We need a God who holds all of human destiny in his hands and has been writing its story for centuries.

When I worked as a television presenter I had the enormous privilege of interviewing Rabbi Hugo Gryn. He hadn't simply survived Auschwitz. He overcame Auschwitz by turning his dreadful experiences into an opportunity to challenge and energise everyone who heard him, in the synagogue, on radio and TV. I asked him where God was in Auschwitz.

He said, 'Wrong question,' and when he saw my consternation, added, 'Let me tell you a story. On the Day of Atonement I went behind the barracks and tried to remember all the familiar prayers. As I stood there praying I began to weep. Then suddenly I became aware of a presence standing next to me, weeping too, so close I could almost reach out and touch him. You ask me where God was in Auschwitz? He was there with his people, suffering with them. The question is, "Where was man in Auschwitz?" '

Adam, where are you? How could the human beings God had made descend to such a level, and how did that make him feel? Rabbi Hugo turned my perspectives upside down. I understood why it was so important to tell the stories of our people from one generation to the next, to look at history as a whole. It gives a sense of continuity and keeps us from despair when times are hard.

We have lost the great tradition of storytelling which Jesus used to such effect. In fact we've lost the Jewish Jesus altogether. In a seminar he calls 'Jesus was a fat man', I heard John Bell of the Iona Community tell of an exercise he inflicts on visitors. He puts images of Jesus up on a wall and asks them to pick the one which most closely reflects their own image of the Son of God. They all choose the pale, thin, 'weight-watchers' Messiah. No one ever opts for the round, cuddly, bouncy Jesus – despite the vast number of references of Jesus eating in the New Testament.

The Pharisees called him a glutton and a wine-bibber. Far be it from me to suggest he was always pogged and plastered, but there is no smoke without fire. He enjoyed his food enormously and knew how to let his hair down at a party. I think he danced. The men did in those days. The good news to one unloved little tax collector was simply, 'Zaccheus, I'm coming to have tea with you.' I wonder whether Mrs Zaccheus was pleased? Not if she was a house-proud Jewish mama taken unawares.

Jesus was a man in touch with his emotions, who told shepherd jokes, laughed at the idea of a man with a log in his eye trying to take the speck out of his companion's eye, kicked the Temple moneylenders' tables over in a fury, wept when he hurt and loved life too much to lay it down easily. His was no stiff British upper lip. But we constantly reduce him to our level.

There's a story about a good sister of the kirk in the last century who went to her minister to complain that the old Queen had been seen rowing on the lake at Balmoral on the Lord's Day. Her minister thought hard and said, 'Ah sister, but did not our Lord row on Lake Galilee on the Lord's Day?' 'That he did, Minister,' she admitted grudgingly, 'But two wrongs don't make a right.'

Jesus was a fully integrated human being – a totally together person without mixed motives and values pulling him in different directions, without neuroses about what was spiritual and what wasn't. We, however, divide our lives into lots of separate little boxes. We chat unreservedly when we meet – until some bright spark opens the meeting in prayer. Then we close our eyes and go into holy mode, as if our praying has suddenly roused the Father from deadly inertia. If only there was a way of acknowledging his unceasing presence.

The great divide is endless. Reading the Bible is spiritual, reading a novel isn't. Going to church is, going to a party isn't. Doing church work is, doing secular work is inferior. Housework is at the bottom of the list. Perhaps when men really get a vision for homemaking and hospitality it will become the most challenging enterprise in the world, requiring a mission statement and strategic planning.

Nowhere are our lives less integrated than in our praying. In a survey in the *Independent*, 70 per cent of the population thought children should be taught to pray – at school. The embarrassment factor of praying at home is just too great. So we hack off the religious bit and only bring it out on special occasions, but that doesn't seem natural and normal to children who see through our little hypocrisies and discomforts.

Then how do we pull ourselves together? The challenge is to find the vertical in the horizontal, the place where God interacts with us in our daily drudgery as individuals and as a community. The Jewish philosophy of life is *halachah*, the way or journey, an ongoing process of discovering God in the most prosaic acts of everyday. To help the process there is a *beracha*, a blessing of God for everything, good, bad and indifferent, the sight of a rainbow, brushing your teeth, even for going to the toilet. We have to do it several times a day, it might as well be a religious experience. That's where I now keep my prayer board, covered in photographs of everyone I love. At least I can guarantee they'll be prayed for regularly.

There seems to be an assumption that home groups are for a cerebral kind of Bible study. The Greeks and Romans revered the mind and engaged in learning for learning's sake. The Jew studies the Torah (which means instruction or teaching, not law) in order to obey. But there's more than one way to absorb God's teaching. Perhaps we could meet occasionally in extended family groups with the children present, perhaps for Sunday lunch, use symbols such as candles, bread and wine, eat together, tell the stories of our people and worship around the table?

All Saints Day could provide a radical alternative party to Halloween, a chance to bring a photo or picture or painting of a saint, biblical or historical, dead or alive, whose testimony helped us on our spiritual journey.

Once again the home, rather than the church building, would become a focal point for worship, while the church, decorated with flowers, balloons and ribbons, could host some grand, rip-roaring celebrations several times a year.

We attempted a Tabernacles instead of harvest this year, a

celebration of God's care of his people during their forty-year stint in the wilderness. We built a huge *succah* in the sanctuary, a frame tent covered in trailing greenery, a symbol of the flimsiness of life on earth. We sang and danced as they did in Jerusalem, we marched around the church waving palm branches, blowing the *shofar* to awaken God's people to warfare and the reality of his imminent return, and we read the words of Jesus spoken on the last day of the feast: 'If anyone thirst let him come to me and drink.' When I invited the congregation to respond to his call, to come and sit under his shelter and receive a fresh outpouring of the latter rain of his spirit, the children came, hand in hand from all over the church and sat in the tabernacle in absolute silence. The sight of it reduced most of us to tears.

Afterwards, at the door, one woman said, 'I'm sorry I couldn't enter in. It's not where I'm at.' I felt unbearably sad for her. The great spiritual sage Henri Nouwen defined celebration as the acceptance that this life is the only one we have and the determination to live it, knowing it is good, for it will be over sooner than we think. This may seem a crazy definition given the suffering in the world. But God commands his people to rejoice on their festivals. Not to do so is gross ingratitude, a sin. That was why a small group of Jews danced in Auschwitz on the Feast of Tabernacles. I don't suppose it was where they were at. It is no coincidence that the African Church, which suffers the most, has the most to teach us about celebration.

It is over thirty years since I became a Christian. As the results of the law of gravity become ever more apparent when I look in the mirror, and I watch my children take over as spiritual leaders, I am more convinced that the life of the church is not expressed by an institution, but by the people of God at home, at work and at play. In fact the institution may well have had its day, though the true church will fight on, underground if necessary.

But this must be a radical, alternative church, offering real freedom in exchange for addictive patterns, real relationships for the hostile and superficial in society, real spirituality for Sunday sham, extended family worship for the brokenness and pain of divorce, community for the alienation on our doorstep, a God who holds the whole of history in his hands for fear and hopelessness, and celebration to banish the despair and disillusionment which beset so many lives. And that, it seems to me, is what rediscovering our roots is all about.

6

My Master and Friend

Colin Urquhart

'Why did God make me?' A typical question of an enquiring eight-year-old! Nobody could give me any kind of satisfactory answer, though. So I had better go to the Creator himself and ask him.

My parents were not believers, so they were not able to help. Why had the question arisen? Although shy and retiring when young, I loved singing and had joined the local church choir. As this was not an evangelical church, I heard nothing of the need to be born again or of the possibility of a personal relationship with Jesus Christ. However, I did hear talk about God being our Creator. Apparently he made me. Hence the question: 'Why?'

Somewhere I had heard that prayer is supposed to be two-way conversation with God. If I prayed, then surely God would answer the question for me! I didn't know how to begin; so I asked my parents to buy me a book of prayers for my birthday, a strange request as far as they were concerned.

The book had three set prayers for each day. Every night I knelt by my bed and read the three prayers diligently, a singularly unexciting activity. However, I had done my part; now it was up to God to do his. Night after night I continued on my knees waiting for him to speak, often falling asleep in the process. My father would see my light on, come and bundle me into bed, but never said anything to me about my nocturnal activities.

I cannot remember hearing God's voice, but every so often it was as if God gave me a sudden, unexpected flash of his glory. Of course, I would not have known how to describe these events at the time; but they were such wonderful occasions that I would kneel by my bedside night after night waiting for the next one. Over a period of time I came to know Jesus; I could put aside the book of prayers and converse directly with him.

Looking back, it seems obvious to me that even in those early years God's hand was upon my life, why I cannot tell. This is the mystery of his election and grace. Instinctively I knew that Jesus loved me, and I can honestly say that ever since I never questioned that love. To me it was the greatest privilege to know that the King of kings had called me to serve him, although I had no idea at first what this would mean.

I was thirteen when the vicar came to me in the choir vestry and told me that the bishop had started a Fellowship of Vocation for those who were contemplating the ordained ministry. The minimum age to belong to this fellowship was sixteen. 'However,' said the vicar, 'it is so obvious that you should be ordained that I have written to the bishop and asked him to make an exception in your case!' Obvious? The thought had never occurred to me! This I had to check out with higher authority! To my surprise the Lord showed me that this was his will for my life.

Eventually I went to King's College, London, at the time the most liberal theological faculty in the country. Only a few months prior to my ordination in 1963 I thought God had made his first mistake in his long career in calling me to be ordained. The thought of having to make many relationships with people I didn't know was so foreign to my nature. If he wanted me to go through with it, he would have to do something, though what I didn't know. I shut myself away in the college chapel one afternoon when I knew nobody else would be around. As I was praying, the Lord suddenly breathed his Holy Spirit into me and I found myself speaking in a strange language. I had no understanding of what was happening. This was before the charismatic movement; I had never heard of anyone being baptised in the Holy Spirit, neither did I have any experience of spiritual gifts. However, from that moment I had the necessary courage to go ahead with the ordination. I knew that God had not given me a spirit of fear, but of power, love and a sound mind.

As a young curate, my responsibility was to visit the sick, the elderly and housebound in the parish. As I did so I found that people were pleased to see me, even though I felt totally inadequate. I had nothing to give them, nothing I could do to alleviate their needs. And there was this small voice inside me that kept saying, 'Heal the sick. Heal the sick.' They had not taught me how to do that at theological college!

The vicar gave me permission to gather a small group together informally to pray and seek the Lord as to how we could heal the sick. News began to spread that such a group existed, and one day one of the housewives in the congregation came to tell me that she had cancer of the bowel. She had already had as much surgery as was possible and nothing more could be done for her medically. Would I pray for her?

'Jesus Christ will heal you,' I said. No sooner were the words out of my mouth than I thought, 'You fool, what have you said?' By the mercy and grace of God, when I did pray for her he wonderfully healed her. She was able to bring up her family and live a full life. News of this healing led to many others asking not only for prayer, but to join further prayer groups for the sick.

Three years later I was put in charge of a district church in Letchworth. While there, another significant development took place in my ministry. I had to preach twice and sometimes three times on a Sunday. I found sermon preparation laborious and time-consuming. And people were very polite about my preaching. 'We know you are trying to say something, Colin, but we are not quite sure what it is!'

Saturday evening arrived one week and I had only had time to prepare my Sunday morning sermon. I went into the church building, locked the door and prostrated myself before the Lord. 'I can't go on like this, Lord. Please speak through me.' I told him that I was going to trust him to give me the words to speak at the evening service.

I led the first part of the service with an increasing sense of unease. I had nothing to say! When it was time for the sermon I prayed the customary prayer and everyone sat down. Still nothing. And then it was as if I was standing beside myself listening. Out of my mouth was coming a flow of words, revelation of things I didn't know or understand myself. To me it was so wonderful that I decided to do the same thing on the following Sunday.

I dutifully prepared my morning sermon and trusted God in the evening. Would the same thing happen again? Throughout the week I was praying that he would once again speak through me, wondering whether such an experience could be repeated. I need not have feared.

During the following weeks the evening congregation doubled and doubled again; but I had no idea why. I told one of the churchwardens, 'I can't understand why all these people are coming.'

'It's the sermons,' he replied, 'in the evenings they are different.'

So others had noticed too! I thought perhaps it was only I who had experienced this flow of revelation every time I preached in this way. I made the decision there and then that this is how I would always prepare to preach, not working out what to say, but being an open channel to enable God to speak through me.

That was thirty years ago; and this is how I have preached ever since, even when speaking at large international conferences.

At first it was tempting on such occasions to think that I should have some kind of prepared text, or at least notes. But this has never worked for me. However, I must make it clear that it is not a matter of simply standing up to speak. My whole life is a preparation to preach, and my time spent with the Lord is essential in order to be an open channel of his grace in this way.

An important part of my time in Letchworth was spent with the young people, at the time the missing age group in church attendance in this country. This was the days of mods and rockers. My counselling room was often my car, parked in the car park of the local pub. One teenager after another would come and sit with me, pouring out his heart, often in desperation. We went on climbing holidays together, and literally saved each other's lives on occasions. So there were deep bonds between us.

The diocesan authorities thought that it was wonderful to have so many young people being confirmed and attending church. We even built our own youth centre and then had to defend it against the gangs that wanted to destroy it. So it was on the strength of this seeming success that I was invited by the bishop to go to St Hugh's, Luton, a parish with a vast new housing estate and many social problems. 'It is so tough,' the bishop told me, 'that we would not leave you there for more than five years.' Both the previous vicars had experienced breakdowns. The job would also include the chaplaincy of the large general hospital, the psychiatric and maternity hospitals, all of which were housed on a complex within the parish. Even though I was only twenty-nine when this offer was made, I would have two curates to assist me.

The prospect was daunting, but when I visited the parish I knew immediately that this was where God wanted me to be, even though I was under no illusions about the seeming success of my time in Letchworth. Yes, the church was full morning and evening. Yes, many young people had come into the church – but more out of respect for me than because they had any kind of dynamic relationship with the Lord. I had poured my life out for these young people, but how many of them really knew, or walked with him? I could not go through this process again. Inside I was crying out for reality. Once again I told the Lord that he would need to do something new in me.

Someone gave me a copy of *The Normal Christian Life* by Watchman Nee, of whom I had never heard. As I read this exposition of Romans 6–8, I found myself saying again and again, 'This is what has happened to me.' At last here was someone explaining to me the significance of what God had done when he filled me with his Holy Spirit just prior to my ordination. I realised that during the six years since then, as I had surrendered certain areas of my ministry to the Lord, the power of his Spirit had infused those areas with life and power, notably in healing and preaching.

Above all, it suddenly hit me that I was a son of God. What had been theory had become heart revelation. I can remember jumping up from my desk and running around the house shouting at the top of my voice, 'I'm a son of God. I'm a son of God.' Fortunately, everyone else was out at the time!

Now I could minister as a son of God, preach as a son of God, heal as a son of God, pray as a son, have the authority of a son, even relate to God the Father as a son, with the boldness and confidence of a son! However, I recognised that I needed wisdom in knowing how to use this new-found faith and authority.

The events of the next few years are described in my first book, *When the Spirit Comes*. They were wonderful years, although very demanding. I could sum up my testimony in one sentence: God continually asking me to do things I couldn't do, and then enabling me to do them! That is the story of my life.

Within about fifteen months virtually the whole of that Anglican congregation had been baptised in the Holy Spirit, although that phrase was never used. It would not have meant anything to us. We were simply a group of people that wanted to be able to communicate the gospel in a meaningful way to all those living in our housing estate. First I had to learn how to teach the people the word of God; and then to show them how to come to genuine repentance by not only receiving forgiveness of their sins, but also by making a complete offering of their lives to the Lord. When we prayed together, we prayed with a naive simplicity: 'Father, please fill this your child with the Holy Spirit in the same way that you filled Peter, Paul and all the apostles.'

Naive or not, it worked! We didn't ask for gifts, but it wasn't long before they came. People began to tell me they found themselves praying with strange words. But the manifestations of healing soon became a focal point. Eighteen different groups met every week to pray for the sick. On Sundays we read out a list of those who had been healed during the previous week, thanking God for his grace. When making an appointment to pray with someone, I would say, 'Let's make a time for your healing.'

Nobody could deny the power of what God was doing. Our first problem was when someone was not healed. People were perplexed. 'How is it possible that we could pray for someone without him being healed?' they asked. I didn't know; I certainly expected everyone to be healed.

News of such things spread fast. This of course was the very beginning of the charismatic movement in this country. At the time there were no books or manuals to consult. It was literally a matter of following the Lord day by day. There was no one else to tell us what to do. It was not long before people were coming from all over the country to meet with God. Pastors hungry for reality in their churches were visiting. Others in need of healing were seeking their personal miracles. Leaders from around the world came to check us out! It was like living in a goldfish bowl. All this puts a great strain on a local congregation. But generally speaking the people coped exceedingly well. It was a great privilege to be in the middle of such a move of God.

My family and I began to live in a large community household in the vicarage. Many people would come, receive their miracle and go on their way rejoicing and praising God. However, there were those who needed to be embraced by a family of love. And even more than the power that was being manifested, it was the love among the members of the church that was an immediate witness to those who visited. We felt we could not send those who came with broken lives back to the situation that either caused or aggravated their problems.

It was not long before we had a houseful of such needy people, twenty in our four-bedroom house. I moved my study into the garage to make a fifth bedroom. At first others did not understand why we were doing this. After some months the penny dropped; all these people were in our home because nobody else was prepared to pay the cost of caring for them. Then more and more people began to help, although on a housing estate the houses were very small and not conducive to such a lifestyle.

We saw many lives changed. Perhaps the most important thing was what I learned in this period by living with people with major emotional problems. I soon discovered that it was not endless counselling they needed, but the truth of God's Word, the truth that Jesus says sets us free! As people learned who they were in Christ and believed that the old had gone, that they really were a new creation, I saw radical changes in their lives. More than this, they learned and applied the principles of faith in their lives. The Word became rock to them, the solid foundation that enabled them to cope with future challenges, without immediately seeking the advice of a counsellor.

At the beginning of this move of his Spirit, the Lord had made clear to me that I was not to think that pastoring this church would be my life's work. 'Your voice will be heard among the nations,' he told me. 'If you do not speak, my people will not hear.' I could not understand what he meant, neither did I want to know at the time. My only objective was to be faithful to him in the situation he had placed me; to be a good pastor to the people under my care; to see more and more people coming to know Jesus personally and having their needs met.

Because of what was happening in the church, I began to be invited to speak at other churches, then at national and international conferences. In 1976 I realised that the Lord was asking me to step out in faith, to trust him for provision and housing and spend my whole time travelling to encourage similar moves of the Spirit in other churches.

As I began to travel I soon realised that what we had been experiencing in Luton was very different from what was called 'renewal'. We had undergone a radical change of lifestyle as we sought to live the life of the kingdom, to lay down our lives in love for others, regardless of the cost. This was very different from wanting experiences, a few gifts and guitars in church.

I had to learn how to minister to large groups of people in a short space of time. They came to meetings with the expectation that many would be born again, baptised in the Holy Spirit and healed, all within the space of a couple of hours. I had learned the need of thorough repentance if people are going to see the power of God in their lives in the way that is necessary; and this added further to the challenge. Every meeting I expected hundreds to be blessed, and they were.

I was hungry for more. In 1980 I, and the team that was working with me, were invited to lead a number of major evangelistic crusades in different parts of the country. Of course we prepared the ground in prayer. For all these crusades we had a simple prayer, 'Lord, please give us your faith for these crusades.'

We had planned a tour of the cities where the missions were to take place, to lead a series of pre-crusade rallies to encourage support among the local churches. As I was preparing for the first meeting the Lord clearly said to me, 'Colin, my faith for these crusades is that you have revival, but you do not believe that.' He was right; it had never occurred to me. In fact I was not altogether sure what revival was!

I read *Finney on Revival* and made a list of over twenty reasons why he maintained churches did not experience continual revival. All on our ministry team began to pray through this list during the following weeks. This led to much repentance, but not revival. The first of these missions was only days away and we certainly did not have what we needed. We could not take revival anywhere unless we had it ourselves!

There was a bank holiday weekend immediately before the first mission. The Lord told us to cancel our plans to have time with our families before the demanding tour began, and to spend the time seeking him. On the Saturday, Jesus walked into the room in his holiness; I cannot explain in any other way what happened. We were all pinned face-down on the carpet for hours as he dealt with us. This was repeated on the following two days, but our lives were radically altered as a result. The housewives and teenagers found themselves praying for up to six hours a day. It was easier to pray than not to pray.

During those crusades, the preaching was different, as were the prayer and ministry times. After preaching, hundreds would run forwards, falling on their knees and faces before God, pouring out their hearts to him. People were coming to the Lord in repentance, being filled with the Holy Spirit and healed without anyone praying for them. I didn't need to minister personally to anyone. I would be prostrate before the Lord on the platform while he performed the ministry.

When this move began, the Lord told me that it would only last for a few months, but was a foretaste of what he was going to do in the nation in the coming years. As I write, it seems that the time for such a move is imminent; we await it with eager expectation. Of course in the intervening years there have been a number of moves, or waves, of the Holy Spirit; but nothing that has had the same spontaneity or depth of holiness.

Our ministry base at the time was at The Hyde, a large country house in Sussex, made available by the Christian owners. For the next three years we had two leaders' conferences there every month, as many pastors and other leaders came to have their lives and ministries impacted by the holiness and power of God.

It became obvious that we needed a training facility to develop this aspect of the work, a Bible college with a true dynamic of revival. A training college called Roffey Place, only five miles from The Hyde, came on the market. Several businesses were interested in this property, but we claimed it for the kingdom. Our bid was accepted because we were the only ones to offer cash! Of course we didn't have any at the time; we would need to see a miracle of God's grace.

Immediately after our bid was accepted, I had to go to Singapore to speak at an Asian Convention. While there I shut myself way with the Lord in my hotel room. I knew that I would only be in a place of genuine faith when I had 'received' the money. Jesus said that whatever we ask for in prayer, we are to believe that we *have* received it, and it would be ours. Believing he will provide is not the same as knowing he has provided!

After about two hours I had a glorious encounter with the Lord, seeing him enthroned in heavenly splendour. He said: 'Colin, I give you a million dollars.' That was all I needed to hear. I got up from my knees and went skipping and dancing around the room, praising God for his goodness.

The next four months proved to be a testing time. Other gifts came in, but not my million dollars; and the legal deadline drew ever closer. I went for a time of ministry in Australia and stopped briefly in Singapore on the way back to England. While having dinner with a friend, who was going to drive me to the airport, he asked how the college project was going. I told him that we had about half the money, but a deadline of only five days to see the Lord supply the rest. He calmly said to me: 'I will see that my bank transfers the money to your bank so that you have it by Friday.' The amount? One million dollars! God is good!

My friend told me that he had given me the money because I had not asked for it! He was tired of Christians asking him for money because they knew he was a successful business man.

These last fifteen years have been a blur for me. For most of the time I have travelled continually, speaking in over forty nations. It seems, though, that God has always wanted to keep us on the cutting edge of things. Whatever God has done in the ministry has come out of the dynamic of the team and students meeting with God on a daily basis back at our base. We have learned the importance of the scriptural command to seek God continually. There are always new things he wants to open up for us, fresh anointing and revelation to give us.

In 1992 Kingdom Faith Church was inaugurated out of a fresh move of God. We had never planted any churches, believing that we were to encourage renewal and revival in existing churches. Now the Lord told us that he wanted us to plant a church that would have definite marks of revival about it, that the time was coming in this nation to build large strategic congregations.

Roffey Place hardly seemed the likely place for such a task, as it is in the middle of countryside, surrounded by fields. We announced that we would hold three weeks of meetings during which we would seek the Lord for a reviving move of his Spirit. The presence and power of God built up night after night, reaching a great climax by the twenty-second night. We took the first group into membership, 230 people. That is not a bad start to a new church; something was obviously happening among us. The church continued to grow rapidly and soon showed its apostolic nature, sending many people out in ministry all over the world. We have been blessed by the continual move of God's Spirit here, particularly in worship. There are times when it seems that the glory of God simply invades the meetings; indescribable!

For the past year I have travelled less, putting more input personally into the church. I have thoroughly enjoyed this and it has been a welcome break from the continual travelling. However, this phase is now coming to a close and the road is summoning again! And of course there are fresh challenges ahead, our new weekly television programme for one, *A Word from God*, to be transmitted on the Christian Channel throughout Europe and beyond.

In between all the activity there have been twenty books

Colin Urquhart

written. People ask me how I manage to write in such a busy schedule. I don't really know the answer. I suppose I always expect to be busy. Jesus is my life. It is no burden to be involved in the work of his kingdom, only a joy and privilege.

In a brief account such as this I cannot speak of all the blessings or, indeed, of all the pain. Of the latter there has been much, just as Jesus promised! Rejection, persecution, deliberate misrepresentation by other Christians, false accusations, every device the enemy can think of to try to hinder fruitfulness for the kingdom.

There have been mistakes on my part too. In retrospect I would have made different decisions at certain points. But it is easy to be wise with hindsight! One thing is certain: I can testify to the continual grace, mercy and love of the Lord Jesus Christ. Whatever has been good and effective has been his grace working through me. The mistakes have been mine.

I am now fifty-nine years old, and the best years are still to come. I live to see all God's promises to me fulfilled, and the most significant ones have yet to be fully realised. I know in my Spirit that the greatest things lie ahead, not in the past. So I will keep seeking the Lord for more effective fruitfulness for his glory. We only have one life here on earth, and I want every day to count.

I have been greatly blessed by my wife, Caroline, my children, Claire, Clive and Andrea and their families; all those who have lived with us over the past thirty years (about 120 different people in all) and by those who have worked closely with me as personal assistants and secretaries. I have been encouraged by those who have shared in leadership in the work, especially Michael Barling who has worked with me for the past twenty years. The corporate nature of our work and anointing at Kingdom Faith cannot be emphasised enough.

My cricketing days lie in the distant past, but I paint as a recreation when I have the opportunity. I cannot sit down and do nothing! Time is too valuable!

Last, I am human! Very human! People want to put platform ministers on a pedestal, the most dangerous place to put anyone. It is so easy to fall off! To me the miracle is that God could take a young person, fearful, inadequate and so ordinary and do extraordinary things in his life. Constantly asking me to do things I cannot do, and then enabling me to do them.

One thing is certain, when serving Jesus life is never boring and is always full. He is a wonderful Master and Friend to have, so loving and kind, patient and generous, faithful and true to his Word; and full of mercy – every day. Praise his wonderful and holy Name!

7

The Reality of Love

Jennifer Rees Larcombe

I lay in my bed, stiff, too afraid to move or call for help – thick darkness seemed to smother me. Beyond my door the floorboards of the old house creaked ominously, convincing me that some monster was stealthily creeping about out there. I was four years old and terribly afraid of the dark. Of course, my mother had often told me that Jesus could hear me even if I called out to him in my head – but was that really true? Tentatively, I tried – and it worked! Outside my thick black curtains, leftovers from the war, a bird began to sing, then another and soon a whole choir had joined them, filling the sinister nocturnal silence with the familiar daytime sounds of a country garden. I had never heard of the dawn chorus. I thought God had put on the show, just for me! That was when I discovered the reality of God.

My parents, Tom and Jean Rees, had bought a ramshackle country mansion at the end of World War 2, and were in the process of converting it into the first Christian conference centre in Britain – Hildenborough Hall. To a small child the vast, echoing house was a terrifying place. My brother and I lived in the nursery with a nanny; our parents were loving but distant –

and always busy. This was hardly surprising with two hundred guests staying with us each week, a staff of thirty-five to manage as well as travelling the world preaching and teaching. In their spare time they wrote forty-six books between them! I adored them both. They were the shining god and goddess who ruled my unusually large world, revered and obeyed by everyone.

'Why *do* we have to have so many visitors?' I remember asking my mother in the car one day.

'They come to find out how to ask Jesus to live in their hearts,' she replied.

'Can I do that?' I asked. I remember it vividly, though I was only four. I will always be glad that my mother replied calmly,

'Yes, of course. Why don't you do it now?' That experience was so real, and remains so clearly in my memory, that no one can convince me small children cannot make that most important of life's decisions.

Early each morning my father used to dress and go down to his study to pray, and that was my cue to snuggle into bed beside my mother. She always had a tray of china tea on her lap – and her battered old Bible. I knew this was her time with God and never attempted to interrupt, but it was my chance to be near her. One morning I suppose she must have been reading Hosea 6, and she began to talk to me about following 'on to know the Lord' (v3, AV).

'Some people ask Jesus into their hearts but they never bother to get to know him,' I remember her explaining. 'Just a few people love him enough to want be as close to him as possible, just like you nestle up to me in the mornings.'

That conversation made a profound impression on me. Another vivid memory must date from that time. I was sitting on a tree stump, somewhere in the lovely, 35-acre garden, and praying my first really fervent prayer.

'Please, I don't want to be just an ordinary Christian, I want to be one of the kind who really follows on to know you.'

Looking back in retrospect at that child on the tree stump, I realise just how important that moment was. I wish I could say that goal has always been my priority, but another goal has run along beside it and often deflected its course.

I clearly recall the 'birth' of that other goal. One night, in the bath, I was furiously angry with my nanny – possibly for no better reason than that she was not my mother! I remember screaming at her and clawing her bare arms until they bled. She must have complained because the following day I was summoned to my father's study.

'Let's take a little walk on the terrace,' he said quietly. It must have been June, because the scent of roses always reminds me of that day.

'Reeses don't behave like you did last night,' he said, as we walked between the rose beds. 'Mummy and I have a very important job to do here, and we need you to help us, because we can't do it unless you're good.'

He was the centre of the universe to me: I would have done anything to please him, so if good behaviour could win his approval – then good I would be. And I was. I can never remember a single other occasion when I was naughty. My hair stands on end now as I write that! Anger and frustration have to go somewhere and so, if strong, negative emotions are buried, rather than acknowledged and expressed appropriately, they do enormous damage.

Of course, my father never meant that conversation to have such an effect on my life, but somehow earning his love and approval became mixed, in my mind, with pleasing God. Father often said he wanted me to serve God full-time when I grew up, so I reckoned that the more successfully I did that, the more I would please him – and God of course!

One day I was playing in my sandpit when my nanny scooped me up and, when she had scrubbed me clean and dressed me in my best frock, she hurried us off to my father's study.

'You're going to meet an emperor,' she hissed, 'so don't forget to curtsy.'

A small, upright gentleman sat stiffly in my father's leather armchair; Emperor Haile Selassie of Ethiopia had come to arrange for his granddaughters to come to stay at Hildenborough. On similar occasions I was summoned to meet such legends as Billy Graham; General Dobbie; Lindsay Glegg; George Scroggie; Mildred Cable; but the one I liked best was Gladys Aylward with her bright, sparrow's eyes and breathtaking stories of adventure. I was far too shy to talk to any of these great spiritual giants who 'dropped in' to see my parents, but oh, how I wanted to be in their league when I grew up.

'I'm sorry, Mrs Rees, but I'm afraid your daughter is backward, educationally subnormal.' Those chilling words were spoken by the fearsome dragon who blighted my school days;[1] I was sentenced to four years 'hard labour' in her form because you only moved up into the next class when you could read. I never mastered the art until I was fourteen. Stories filled my head but when I tried to transfer them on to paper, the words were a jumbled mess, and the teacher would write 'gibberish' right across the page.

Nowadays my problems might have been labelled 'dyslexia' and received specialist help, but in those days I just hid in the back row, the target for the endless taunts of a spiteful teacher and classmates who followed her lead and added their jeers to hers. By eleven I was so traumatised my parents allowed me to stay at home, and a series of governesses completed my embarrassingly scanty education.

Looking back on my teenage years I can see I became alarmingly withdrawn, so shy I would only go out during the holidays when my much-loved brother was home from boarding-school. A terrible sense of failure and embarrassment haunted me because I 'wasn't clever enough to go to school'. I only felt happy and safe alone in my bedroom. I must have been a terrible disappointment to my parents. Yet it was in the absence of friends, school and all the other activities which fill the lives of normal adolescents that God made himself real to me in such a beautiful way that my memories of those days are immensely happy. I literally spent hours praying, and my motivation for finally learning to read was in order to understand the big, black, leather Bible my father gave me for my fourteenth birthday.

I was sixteen when I finally 'came out' of prison. My father was conducting a nationwide evangelistic campaign, known as the Mission to Britain, which entailed preaching at several centres in every single county of the British Isles over a period of nine months. My parents asked me to go on the adventure with them.

Oh, the fun of it! And what a lesson in geography the adventure gave me – seeing Britain from the Isle of Wight to the Outer Hebrides, from Londonderry to the flat wastes of Norfolk. I heard my father preach night after night, in churches of every denomination and to vastly differing congregations, and I never got over the thrill of hearing him explain the cross. I was always moved to tears at the sight of people streaming forward to confess their new-found faith in Christ. It was probably as good a training as I would have received in any Bible college, and it certainly began to build my self-confidence.

The Mission to Canada followed when I was eighteen, and when my father was unable to take a youth service one evening, he calmly announced that 'his daughter would speak instead'. The church was packed with several hundred people and how could a painfully shy teenager possibly stand up in front of them all? As I hid, terrified, in the vestry, just before the dreaded moment, I was conscious of something descending on me. It felt like warm treacle pouring down from my head to my feet. As I stepped into the pulpit, a totally new person began to speak. My words sounded confident, even authoritative, and the congregation never moved a muscle throughout my talk. Now, I realise that treacle was 'God's anointing'. To this day I am still as terrified before I speak, but when his anointing comes down over me the mouse, which is the real me, is possessed by a powerful lion. As I watched the faces of my first congregation, and saw them moved by the message God was giving them through me, I renewed that secondary vow of mine to serve God for the rest of my life.

Perhaps the only time I ever deliberately displeased my father was when I fell in love with a big, blond schoolteacher called Tony. When you think of how much I suffered at the hands of the teaching profession it does seem strange that I should fall in love with one of them! I poured out my feelings to him in a passionate love letter, which he returned the following day, with all my spelling mistakes carefully corrected in red ink – but I still married him!

We lived in an ordinary little house in an ordinary little village, and he went to work every day from nine to four in an ordinary school. After my totally abnormal life, that ordinariness was delightful. We soon began to have children with embarrassing frequency, until our quiver contained six. I adored the big, kindly man who introduced me to the real world, and then rebuilt me. It was Tony who turned me into a writer by encouraging me to write down the stories I told the children. When they were in bed, I climbed into the attic and banged them out on an ancient typewriter. Then Tony would get out his famous red pen and correct the spellings so I could type them all over again but, to my astonishment, the publishers seemed to like them.

Being blissfully happy in a country village with a husband I adored and a healthy family to bring up, not to mention a career in writing, still left me with the niggling feeling I was falling short of God's plans for me. I felt driven towards the 'great life's work' I was convinced he required of me. Wherever we lived I worked frenziedly, organising evangelistic events, children's missions, youth groups; and the house was constantly filled with people in need. I am not belittling all that, people were definitely blessed through my activities, but it is *why* I did those things which I question now. We need to serve God as part of our relationship of love and trust, not in order to win his affection, or to fulfil someone else's dreams.

Perhaps because I was so happily married I began to find that close relationship I had with God, as a lonely teenager, gradually dying away. Tony was totally capable and made me so completely happy that I no longer needed to rely on God to meet all my needs. He had become a Master to be served rather than a Father to be loved and relied upon.

One morning, just before my youngest son was due to start school, I found myself wide awake at five o'clock. I was not sure what had woken me, but I sensed it was God himself. I felt him clearly say, 'Anna the prophetess', so I went downstairs, made a mug of tea and opened my Bible at Luke 2. Why did this obscure OAP suddenly feel so significant to me? Then I sensed God was telling me he wanted me to be a prophetess, like Anna. For the next few days I sailed through life, ten feet off the ground. At last! All those years of motherhood and organising church activities had merely been my training period. Now, at last, I was going to become the high-powered evangelist who toured the world by jet-plane – just like my father.

Finding myself, soon afterwards, in an ambulance being rushed into hospital, seriously ill with a brain virus, was the very last thing that I expected. For months I was separated from my family and when I finally returned home, the virus had left me disabled in many ways. I was in constant pain, muscular weakness prevented me from walking more than a step or two and I had no sense of balance. As it gradually dawned on me that my chances of recovery were very slight, I wondered how I could be a prophetess in a wheelchair and I began to feel God had deceived me. He seemed to have taken the life I had confidently offered to him, and chucked it carelessly away on the scrapheap.

The next two years seem very bleak as I look back on them.[2] I was convinced God still healed people, He had even used my hands to do so and several people would testify to that. Yet, in spite of prayer, fasting, calling the elders and attending countless healing services, I did not recover. What was I doing wrong? Both my parents were dead by that time, but I would have given anything for a lengthy conversation with my father. He would have known how to extricate me from this mess – even if God didn't seem interested.

It really was my 'dark night of the soul' with everything disintegrating around me. I was no longer able to be an active mum or the 'hub' of the church and village activities; my marriage was rocking, and the children's 'difficult' behaviour reflected their distress. 'What price Anna now!' I wrote furiously in my journal. I was nothing but a burden on society, a number in a DSS file, and I longed for the courage to kill myself.

It is so easy *now* to see that 'in all things God works for the good of those who love him' (Romans 8:28), but I didn't think so at the time! If only I had realised he was planning a special, if rather messy, appointment with me – which certainly changed my life. Anyone who has ever met me has heard me tell the story of how I fell in the cow-dung, but I must repeat it because it was such a turning point.[3] On a Saturday morning when life seemed at its blackest, I shuffled myself out into the garden on my elbow crutches in order to scream – loud and long. Instead I over-balanced and fell in a lake of manure which had seeped in from the field over the hedge. I was quite unable to get up, however much I struggled and, feeling that the disgusting sludge symbolised the mess my 'beautiful' life had become, I began to tell God just what I thought of him! He could have prevented all the disasters, which plagued us, if only he had responded to all those prayers and healed me.

Suddenly, at the height of my tirade, he was there with me, right in the middle of the filthy dung. I have never felt so totally loved as I did at that moment. He wanted me to want just him, not healing, or a great ministry, just him and him alone. I was so amazed I simply asked him to come right back into the centre of my existence and gave him leave to do what he liked with me.

The next six years were rich and delightful. My health continued to deteriorate, I was frequently in hospital and soon dependent on a wheelchair, but my relationship with God moved into a new dimension – he was no longer a hard to please Father or an exacting Master; he became a friend and companion. Looking again at the verses about Anna the prophetess, I realised her 'public utterances' arose out of years spent in God's presence – getting to know him, as Paul did, by sharing the fellowship of suffering (Philippians 3:10).

The treasures of darkness (Isaiah 45:3) are immensely valuable and I began to pass them on to others through the books I wrote during those years.[4] I could only type when I was lying almost flat, with my arms supported by pillows, and Tony replaced the old typewriter with my first computer. All the members of our family recall the sense of wellbeing and peace we enjoyed during those years, which I believe were God's special gift to us.

After nearly eight years of illness, however, my old discontent returned (or as I preferred to call it then, my zeal) and the 'other goal' began to drive me again. By this time, *Beyond Healing* had become a bestseller, appreciative letters arrived from all over the world and I began to speak in public again, sitting in my wheelchair. If only I could have a more powerful anointing, I thought, and if God was not going to heal me, then at least he could give me back that gift of healing for others.

In August 1989 we went for a holiday to the Lake District. I knew how much blessing God had poured out in the past over the little town of Keswick so, when we were staying there, I felt it was a fitting place to ask for my heart's desire. One afternoon, in the pouring rain, I went out by myself in my battery-operated wheelchair, and sat looking out over Derwent Water.

'Lord,' I prayed, 'give me more power in my ministry and more gifts of your Holy Spirit so I can serve you more effectively.' Somehow I felt he was not listening so the following week, when we had travelled to Devon in search of the sun, I asked him again. This time I was sitting by the sea, watching the children playing on a sandy beach where my wheelchair could not follow. Suddenly I was convinced Jesus himself was standing on the large red rock which jutted out into the sea. His presence was so tangible I could hardly breathe, but I still found the audacity to repeat my request. This time there was a distinct answer.

'All you need is me.' Just five short words, which have formed another landmark in my life, but at the time they were definitely *not* what I wanted to hear.

Every time I drive up the M4 motorway I remember the spot where, on the way home from that holiday, I asked God why he had not granted my request.

'You couldn't handle it' was his reply, and I distinctly remember arguing, 'Why not give me the chance to prove that I could?' I have often wondered how different life might have been for all of us if I had never prayed that prayer!

A few months later, through the prayers of a new Christian, I was suddenly and totally healed and left my wheelchair behind forever.[5] It is hard to describe what an enormous difference that made to our family. Almost overnight I possessed the ministry for which I had always longed. Invitations to speak came from all over the world, chances to speak on TV and radio and endless requests from publishers and editors. For the next six years I travelled, spoke and wrote for God enthusiastically. Tony left education to work with me, and the Lord really did pour out the warm treacle of his anointing over us both. Because of our struggles during the first few years of my illness we both longed to help others who were trying to adjust to terminal and chronic illness – or indeed, loss of any kind.[6] So we began running holidays and retreats for them in this country and abroad.

The administration kept Tony increasingly based at home with our two youngest boys, who were in their last years at school, while I dashed from one engagement to the next. And I loved every minute of it. Here I was, doing just the kind of job my father would have wanted for me, but I guess I was really doing it to please him, and not out of love for God at all. When a ministry keeps you very busy it is possible to live on stored spiritual fat for a time, but should that ministry continue to rob you of time and energy to press into God and seek him for his own sake, then you are in danger. The very thing, which is your passion and your greatest gift from God, can so easily become an idol that replaces him at the centre of your being. Fortunately he never tolerates that for long!

Our holidays and retreats became so popular they were too crowded to be fully effective. So we began to see the need to work with people individually or in far smaller groups. This led us to search for somewhere in the country where people, grappling with loss, could come and spend time with us. In the Kentish hills we found a bungalow, surrounded by a lovely garden; and with the generous help of friends, we started to build a prayer room on the side of it, with facilities for the disabled. In our minds was the vision of a miniature healing centre. I was beginning to realise my travelling ministry was becoming far too important to me, and I missed Tony so badly when I was away; we both felt a more home-based life would be better.

Then everything began to go wrong! Our Christian builder went broke while the extension was still only a skeleton, plunging us into serious financial problems. Tony's elderly mother had a stroke and, because she needed our constant care, she came to live with us. I suddenly became unwell, and the surgeon told us bluntly that he was investigating cancer. The subsequent surgery went badly wrong, leaving me with serious, ongoing pain and infection.

During a prayer meeting in our home, I remember asking God why he was making life so difficult when all I wanted was to be used by him. His reply was a picture of a large orange. I saw it distinctly. Then I also saw a sharp knife cut it in half and two huge hands squeezing the sweet juice into a bowl. The Lord seemed to say, 'Your life is like this orange – at its most useful when it is cut open and crushed to release nourishment for others.'

About that time I began to realise something strange was happening to Tony. He seemed to be dying spiritually, losing interest in our work and particularly in his faith. Soon I discovered he had fallen in love with a lady we were counselling, who is much younger and more attractive than I am. For months he struggled with temptation but finally he left to live with her. For thirty years I thought our marriage was happy and fulfilling, so the shock and grief I felt, as I watched him drive away down the lane, is quite indescribable. All I wanted, and still want, is for him to come home.

Once again life seemed to be disintegrating; the last of our large brood left home for university just two weeks before Tony's departure, ending twenty-nine years of enjoyable motherhood. My trustees cancelled all my speaking engagements and all the retreats we had planned, very wisely, but I doubted if anyone would ever ask a woman whose marriage had failed to speak in public again. If we had to sell the house, our plans for a healing centre were also finished. It felt as if I had lost everything and everyone.

I honestly did not think I could survive without Tony. He had been the practical one, fixing everything that went wrong, and handling all the business side of our lives. I had never even had a bank account and such things as mortgage repayments, direct debits and council tax were a complete mystery to me. I did not even know how to use a bank card to obtain cash! I doubt if there has been a feebler wife since Queen Victoria died!

One horrible winter night, a few months after Tony left, I was curled up on the sofa, too miserable and afraid to go to bed. The bungalow, which had seemed ideal because of its country setting, suddenly felt isolated, hemmed in by eerie woods and long dark lanes. A storm outside produced all kinds of sinister noises which terrified me; my desk was piled with forms I couldn't understand and bills I could not pay; the loo had flooded the bathroom floor and, worst of all, there was a mouse in my bedroom cupboard.

A ghastly sense of abandonment overwhelmed me – closely followed by such a feeling of failure and shame I wished I were dead. Why had I been too busy and blind to notice our marriage was not as stable as I thought it had been?

Then I remembered a card a friend had sent me that morning with a message scrawled inside. 'Take a look at Isaiah 54.' I felt too depressed to bother but, in order to pass the time, I opened my Bible. Here are the words which 'hit' me in the eye.

> 'Do not be afraid; you will not suffer shame ... For your Maker is your husband – the Lord Almighty is his name ... you were a wife deserted and distressed in spirit ... a wife who married young, only to be rejected,' says your God ... 'Though the mountains be shaken and the hills be removed, yet my unfailing love for you will not be shaken.'

I knew the ideal Old Testament husband was his wife's protector, provider and spiritual teacher, and from him she derived her status in the world. He was also responsible for her welfare and happiness, to a degree which is hard for us to comprehend. By saying he was my husband, God seemed to be offering me a far deeper and more intimate relationship than that of a father or a friend; the closest alliance of all – when two merge and become one flesh (Genesis 2:24).

'Surely the symbol only applied to Israel?' I argued with myself. 'No, there were all those New Testament references to Christians being the bride of Christ. Wasn't he talking about a collective relationship, applying to a whole nation?' I was still struggling! Then I realised that most of the references to God being a father were addressed to Israel or the church as a whole, yet we always think of him as our personal Heavenly Father as well.

By standing in a husband's place, God was taking responsibility for all my practical and emotional needs – for the rest of my life. All I had to do was accept his offer by deciding to trust him.

Slowly, over the next few weeks, my 'husband' helped me sort through those confusing forms. He sent a friend to mend the loo and the leaking roof. He made it possible for me to keep my home, and I don't know what he did about the mouse, but I never saw it again!

But far more important than all these practical things, he has also given me a deep sense of being loved and valued – not for what I do, or even for who I am – but just because I'm *me!* Recently, at the end of a Sunday service, I saw a couple standing close together at the back of our church. The wife was upset because their daughter was going abroad, and when she began to cry her husband wrapped his arms round her so tenderly a pang of grief shot through me.

'I have no one to hold or comfort me like that,' I thought. Somehow I sensed the Lord was gently tapping me on the shoulder.

'You're here in church with *your* husband too,' he seemed to say, 'and I love you far more than any earthly husband ever could.' Since then the wonder of his eternal and unconditional love keeps hitting me with fresh new force! When I think how often I have explained to audiences, all over the world, just what Jesus did for us on the cross it does seem strange that only recently have I discovered the full extent of what he did for me! All those mistakes, 'if onlys' and wrong motives can be deleted without trace through the power of his sacrifice!

Even with the reality of love like that, the feeling of disgrace you experience when your marriage fails takes you completely by surprise. My instinct was to retreat to some remote cottage and keep out of the public eye, but I was reading one of Leanne Payne's books one day when the Lord seemed to pick a phrase off the page and hand it to me. 'Lord, transform this agony into healing power for others.' There are so many other people out there in this harsh world who have to go through the kind of things I've experienced, but without knowing about the love Jesus has for them or his ability to comfort and rebuild their lives. Perhaps they would not receive this good news so easily from a happily married, healthy individual as they might from someone who has experienced similar pain and loss.

Somewhere inside me there is still the child who sat on the tree stump and yearned to know God, to nestle into him as closely as possible. But what about the other child, who vowed to serve him well enough to win approval? Well, I hope she is safely laid to rest for ever. Yet, I am convinced that the contemplative, peaceful 'Mary' and the active, hardworking Martha who struggle for control in most of us can work together, so long as they are held in balance. We can know deep intimacy with God while, at the same time, we are busily serving him but we can only do this when our greatest goal is to know, love and please God. When that desire leads the rest, the others fall into place comfortably behind it.

So I face a new millennium, feeling bruised and broken, rather like that orange, with no self-confidence left at all, but I'm clinging tightly to the Lord's hand. He is all I need, and I'm ready to move, with him, into the next leg of my journey home – whatever it may hold.

1. I have written more fully about my school experiences in *Turning Point* (Hodder & Stoughton, 1994).
2. I have described this period of my life fully in *Beyond Healing* (Hodder & Stoughton, 1986).
3. See *Unexpected Healing* (Hodder & Stoughton, 1991).
4. *Where Have You Gone, God?* (Hodder & Stoughton, 1989); *Beyond Healing; No Hands but Ours* (HarperCollins).
5. *Unexpected Healing.*
6. *Turning Point.*

8

Loving God with Mind
and Heart

Alister McGrath

One of the childhood experiences which I recall most vividly was lying awake on my bed at night, looking out of a window towards the stars. I was a boarder at the Methodist College, Belfast, aged about fourteen. Like so many people of that age, I was fairly sure that I knew everything that mattered, and had all the great issues of life sorted out. Back in the 1960s, most young people seemed to assume that religion was a waste of time. Marxism was much more attractive – and relevant! I was going to be a research scientist, and sort out the problems of the world through new cures for diseases.

Yet the certainties on which my life was grounded were slowly being eroded. One of the issues which troubled me was the question of mortality. What was the point of life? It seemed so brief and insignificant. Looking at the stars increased my sense of despondency. I knew that some of the stars I was observing were so far away that their light took hundreds of years to reach me. This meant that I would be dead before the light now being emitted by those stars would reach the earth. I found it a disturbing thought. The classic way of dealing with such thoughts, of course, is to ignore them, and hope that they will go away. Yet this particular thought, and an increasing number of their cousins, refused to go away.

My own discovery of the Christian faith took place when I was eighteen, late in 1971. I had gone up to Oxford University to study natural sciences. At an intellectual level, I still regarded myself as a Marxist, although subtle doubts had begun to creep in. Wadham College then had a modest reputation as a centre of Marxist thinking, and attracted a number of left-wing students in consequence. My own reasons for attending at this time probably had more to do with its outstanding chemistry tutors – such as Jeremy R. Knowles and R. J. P. Williams – than its political climate.

Looking back on that time of my life, it is clear that my early rejection of Christianity was based on a misunderstanding. My outlook on life was shaped by my reactions to what I can now see was a caricature. Perhaps that caricature was ideally suited to the needs of a schoolboy, who wanted quick answers to complex questions. The doubts about the credibility of my Marxist outlook began to resurface and – like Augustine in the cathedral at Milan – I would attend Christian meetings in my attempt to discover what it was all about. University was a place at which one had time to think about life more critically than before, and I came to the conclusion that I had misjudged and misunderstood Christianity.

It would be foolish and quite inaccurate to say that this sorted everything out. In one sense, it opened a door on a new set of questions, many of which I was poorly equipped to answer. Conversion is perhaps one of the most unsettling experiences of life. All of one's certainties are swept away, and one has to begin thinking all over again. Old questions needed new answers; I had to wrestle with questions which had never troubled me before. How can the existence of a loving God be reconciled with the existence of sin in the world? Or, perhaps a little less abstractly and more urgently, what should I do with the rest of my life?

Faced with new questions, it is fatally easy to provide quick and easy answers – answers which may offer temporary fixes, but which are quite inadequate as long-term solutions. Like so many Christians in the first stages of their growth, I found myself occasionally puzzled and sometimes more than a little distressed by some of the answers provided by well-meaning Christian friends (who often seemed to know as little about their faith as I did) and some of the visiting speakers at the university Christian Union, who seemed to think that the hallmark of Christian authenticity was a studied refusal to think about their faith. We were asked to trust the speakers, and that seemed to be about as far as it went.

I do not think that I was ever tempted to give up my new-found faith on account of the shallowness of some of these presentations. Nevertheless, I was quite convinced that there had to be more intellectual substance to the Christian faith than I had found in student Christianity. I regularly found myself sneaking home to read C. S. Lewis, whose discussions of difficult issues seemed incalculably more satisfactory than those offered elsewhere.

I do not mean to be totally negative about those who offer these quick fixes to Christian students, who are often at a very early stage in their Christian lives and need a lot of patience, care and love. Nor am I dismissing out of hand their demand to accept their ideas as truth, rather than think about it. It is, however, fair to point out that many of these young lives of faith will later become shipwrecked on the rocks of precisely those questions to which inadequate answers were given – yet they were discouraged from seeking better ones out of some misguided belief that this reflected a lack of trust in God.

It became clear to me that I wanted to study the Christian faith in depth. This annoyed the 'don't think – trust!' people.

This didn't trouble me unduly. As someone who was studying science, I was particularly interested in thinking more deeply about the relation of Christianity and the natural sciences. Nevertheless, it had become clear to me that there was another need that I was increasingly aware of – the need to *explain* the ideas of Christianity. Young Christians – and here I had my own experience in mind as much as anything – needed to be reassured that the leading ideas of the Christian faith made sense; that they rested on secure foundations; and that the Christian faith would be impoverished and compromised if they were *not* here. In short, I became aware of the need for *the explanation, justification and appreciation of Christian teachings.*

I was not really able to do much about this until I was ordained into the ministry of the Church of England in 1980. I initially spent three years at a parish in the suburbs of Nottingham (St Leonard's, Wollaton), where I was able to incorporate a substantial amount of my developing thinking on the explanation, justification and appreciation of Christian themes into sermons and talks. I was especially glad to have been involved in youth work at this time, as it allowed me to try out a wide range of approaches on people aged sixteen, seventeen and eighteen. I was then invited to return to Oxford to teach at Wycliffe Hall, one of the Church of England's leading theological colleges, which prepares men and women for ministry in that church and beyond. It offered me marvellous opportunities to develop my thinking and teaching on these important themes.

Finally, I began to publish my ideas. The very warm response to the books in question brought home to me how important it was to reassure people of the integrity and resilience of their faith. It is a lesson that has remained with me, and which continues to challenge and excite me. My most recent book to adopt this style is *Theology for Amateurs* (Hodder and Stoughton, 1999), which illustrates my approach very well.

I do not think that my understanding of the basic doctrines of the Christian faith has developed significantly in the last ten years. I remain a firm supporter of what C. S. Lewis termed 'mere Christianity' and have little interest in the boundary disputes which so frequently break out between different styles of Christians. This is not to say that I have ceased to think about my faith, in that there has unquestionably been development in my understanding of the gospel.

In the last ten years, I have come to appreciate more of the immense spiritual and intellectual richness of the Christian gospel. This has not come about through any doctrinal changes, but through an increased awareness of the implications of my faith for various areas of life. In the remainder of this piece, I would like to explore some areas in which I have found my faith deepening.

The first such area is the doctrine of creation. Like many evangelical Christians, the doctrine of redemption has always been close to my heart. It is impossible for any of us to fully grasp the wonder of God's saving love for us in Christ, and I, in common with many others, find reflection on this great theme immensely challenging and stimulating. However, I became aware that my emphasis on the great work of God in redemption had caused me to overlook the doctrine of creation. The God who redeems us, after all, is the same God who creates us. To explore the doctrine of creation is not for one moment to lessen any commitment to the joy, wonder and importance of redemption. It is like holding a different facet of the jewel of the Christian faith up to the light, and realising that there is more to the Christian faith than we had first appreciated.

Although I had always been aware that God creates the world, I had not paid much attention to this aspect of my faith. Rediscovering the doctrine of creation is about allowing the vastness, intricacy and glory of the world to remind us of the wisdom and glory of its creator. I found these ideas being echoed in the great hymn of St Patrick, patron saint of my native Ireland:

> I bind unto myself today
> The virtues of the star-lit heaven,
> The glorious sun's life-giving ray,
> The whiteness of the moon at even,
> The flashing of the lightning free,
> The whirling wind's tempestuous shocks,
> The stable earth, the deep salt sea,
> Around the old eternal rocks.

The same idea is also found in the work of the great eighteenth-century Puritan writer Jonathan Edwards, who found his enjoyment of God's world immeasurably enhanced by meditating on the doctrine of creation.

> The Son of God created the world . . . to communicate himself in an image of his own excellency . . . He communicates a sort of shadow . . . of his excellencies . . . so that when we are delighted with flowery meadows and gentle breezes . . . we may consider that we see only the emanation of the sweet benevolence of Jesus Christ.

This new interest in the doctrine of creation is also of importance to my professional work as a Christian theologian. One of my particular areas of interest is the relation between the Christian faith and the natural sciences. The doctrine of creation is of immense importance here, for several reasons. It establishes that there is a God-given order to the world, which the natural sciences are able to discern. I find it helpful to think of there being three aspects to the relevance of Christian faith to the natural sciences.

1. Creation concerns the establishment of ordering and coherence within the world.
2. The ordering or coherence within the world can be regarded as expressing or reflecting the nature of God himself.
3. The creation can thus be seen as pointing to God, in that

the exploration of its ordering or coherence leads to an understanding of the one who ordered it in this manner.

Perhaps it should not surprise us that so many natural scientists are Christians, contrary to the stereotype which Richard Dawkins and others would like us to accept – namely, that the sciences are implacably opposed to faith in God.

A second area in which I found my faith developing relates to the area of spirituality. Many evangelical Christians still have difficulty with the term 'spirituality', pointing out that it is not biblical. I can certainly agree with this concern. But, in fairness, we use countless words to describe aspects of our Christian lives that are not found in the Bible. For example, most of my working life is taken up with teaching theology. Now 'theology' is a perfectly respectable word, and is used without hesitation by evangelicals. Yet it is not a biblical term.

In reality, this causes no significant problems. Ever since the fourth century, Christians have accepted the use of non-biblical terms to refer to thoroughly biblical notions. The practice has long since ceased to be controversial. I see no difficulty with using the term 'spirituality' to refer to and to express some of the great biblical insights concerning the impact of faith upon our existence. The important thing is to make sure that our approaches to spirituality are focussed on Christ and grounded in Scripture.

In my first period as a Christian, I found my attention focussing on *understanding* my faith. I continue to regard this as being of the utmost importance. There is a marvellous coherence to Christian doctrine, and wrestling with the great truths of our faith provided me with both spiritual encouragement and intellectual challenge. Yet it seemed to me that my 'knowledge' of the Christian faith was rather dry and cerebral.

Part of the difficulty was that I was, like most people of my generation, deeply influenced by the Enlightenment. Christianity was all about *ideas* – and it was important to get those ideas right. As a result, theological correctness had become something of an obsession with me. I had failed to realise that the gospel affects every level of our existence – not just the way we think, but the way in which we *feel* and *live*. The Enlightenment had championed the role of reason, and vetoed any engagement with emotions or imagination. Yet I knew that writers such as Jonathan Edwards and C. S. Lewis had stressed the importance of precisely these aspects of our lives. I gradually came to the realisation that my faith was far too academic. I needed to discover something which I had improperly suppressed.

My realisation of the importance of spirituality began about 1989, but really blossomed from about 1992. I was invited to lead a regular summer school course in Oxford on 'medieval and Reformation spirituality'. This allowed me to engage with some of the great texts of Christian spirituality. As my students and I wrestled with these texts, we found ourselves challenged to deepen the quality of our Christian faith through being more open to God. I found that the quality of my Christian life deepened considerably as a result.

I also found myself wanting to explore how others had grasped the importance of spirituality, and so found myself being drawn to writing a biography of J. I. Packer, widely regarded as one of evangelicalism's most distinguished theologians, who stressed the importance of theology to spirituality, and vice versa. Researching and writing that biography (which took five years) helped me appreciate both the importance of this theme, and also the considerable personal contribution which Packer had made to its discussion and application. It also helped me understand more of the history of evangelical Christianity in England and the United States in the second half of the twentieth century.

As I mentioned earlier, my basic understanding of Christian doctrine has not changed over the last ten years. I remain deeply committed to the fundamentals of Christian orthodoxy. What has happened is that these ideas have taken on a new depth, both as I appreciated more their implications, and as I realised that my grasp of the totality of the Christian gospel had been shallow. Perhaps I could say that I experienced a deepening in the quality of my faith, rather than any change in what I believed.

Traditional theology makes a distinction between two senses of the word 'faith'. On the one hand, there is the 'faith which believes' – that is, the personal quality of trust and commitment in God. On the other, there is the 'faith which is believed' – that is, the body of Christian doctrine. Using this way of speaking, I could say that, in my case, the 'faith which is believed' remained unaltered. What developed, matured and deepened was the 'faith which believes'. The New Testament often compares the kingdom of God to a growing plant, or a seed taking root. What happened to me was that a plant which had grown to some extent underwent a new spurt of growth, leading to increased strength and vitality. I try to convey something of what I had discovered in *The Journey* (Hodder and Stoughton, 1999), which aims to show how the Christian journey was both illuminated and assisted by reading Scripture in depth, rather than superficially.

Why am I writing this? I doubt if anyone will be especially interested in my personal life of faith. But it may be that some reading this chapter will feel that they can identify with my earlier and rather academic approach to faith, and are fed up being told by their doubtless well-meaning friends that they just need to know more *facts* about their faith. My experience is that we need to *go deeper*, rather than just *know more*. Perhaps we all have to discover that we have simply scratched the surface of the immense riches of the gospel. Beneath the surface lies so much more, which we are meant to discover and enjoy. The greater our appreciation of the wonder, excitement and sheer delight of the Christian faith, the more effective our witness to our friends, and the greater our enjoyment of the Christian faith.

Enjoyment? Yes! 'What', asked the *Shorter Westminster Catechism*, 'is the chief end of man?' The answer given is rightly celebrated as a jewel in Christianity's doctrinal crown: 'to glorify God and enjoy him for ever'. This brief statement sets us on a journey of personal exploration – to gain a fresh apprehension of the glory of God, so that we might return that glory to God and have our spiritual lives enriched by the knowledge of such a God. To catch such a glimpse of the full splendour of God is also a powerful stimulus to evangelism. Was it not by catching a glimpse of the glory of God in the temple that Isaiah responded to the divine call to go forth in service? Good theology is essential to mission and evangelism! By catching a vision of God in all his radiance and glory, we long to serve him now and finally be with him in the New Jerusalem.

So what do I think will happen in the next decades? To be honest, I don't know – and I'm not that sure that I need to. I have always taken the view that we don't need to see the big picture. The important thing is to get on with whatever work God has entrusted to us, and trust him in return. And that's what I intend to do. Becoming a Christian was the best thing, humanly speaking, that I ever did, and it is a landmark in my life. The important thing now is to keep on loving and serving God, whatever lies ahead.

9

When Life Crumbles
Lesley Bilinda

'How can you still believe in God after all that's happened to you? I'd give up on Christianity if I were you.'

The suggestion made a lot of sense. It was made by a friend who was not a Christian, but was nonetheless deeply concerned about the horrors happening in Rwanda and elsewhere. She was not mocking, but genuinely concerned for me, and mystified as to how I could continue believing in a God of love, when all around me was pain and suffering. It was clear to her that my Christian faith was actually making matters even more complicated for me as I struggled to make any sense out of the situation.

Perhaps she was right. Perhaps it would be easier just to leave God out of the picture altogether. After all, he seemed to be having no effect in stopping the genocide in Rwanda, and felt so far away at the very time when I needed him most.

But it was not so easy just to turn my back on God. He had been a part of my life for as long as I could remember. Could I now just drop him completely? And what was the alternative? No one else seemed to have any better explanation for the chaos around. But on the other hand, how could I carry on believing in a religion which seemed to work only sometimes and not other times? If Christianity were true, it had to be so as much when life crumbles as when it is rosy. It had to make sense of the hardest questions of life. There was no room for niceties and platitudes. I wanted tough answers to the horrors that were being thrown into my face. If God had no answers, there would be no point in continuing. But if he did have answers, it would be impossible to turn away.

Could my earlier experiences of God shed any light on the situation now? Where did it all begin?

Beadles and black robes

Since I was knee-high to a grasshopper I had been a faithful attender at the local church. Born into the traditions of Scottish Presbyterianism, church for me as a small child was a solemn affair. We all went as a family Sunday by Sunday, as did so many families in the small town in which I grew up. It just seemed to me to be part of the routine – much the same as the Brownies and piano lessons. The large town centre church was somewhat musty-smelling and dim inside despite the massive stained glass windows, and made even more sombre by the long black robes of both the beadle and the minister. I knew God was around somewhere, but not very near, probably wore a long black robe and didn't smile much – especially if I forgot to say my prayers any evening.

Major rebellion was not exactly the characteristic of my teenage years, but after faithfully progressing through many years of Sunday school, my small stab at an adolescent protest resulted in my refusal to continue with the next step – Bible class. It was not so much an anti-God stance as an embarrassment because the Bible class leader was my father. Not an easy situation for a young teenager! Actually, it was a convenient let-out since church had begun to feel boring and irrelevant. But this mild rebellion was not to last long.

The crunch came a couple of years later at a young people's summer Christian camp. Surrounded by enthusiastic, happy new friends, I began to see a different side to Christianity, personal and dynamic – something I had not previously encountered – and it intrigued and challenged me. So much so that by the end of the week I realised that God did not have to be far off with a grim face, but could be known personally through Jesus. So it was decided. I prayed the prayer at the end of the final meeting and gave my life to Jesus. This was exciting! I had to get home and tell my parents that for all these years they had got it wrong; that they had never told me what it meant *really* to be a Christian.

Oops! Not a good move. In fact, a very tactless and insensitive move. It was a thoughtless rejection of everything my parents had stood for, and hurt them deeply. Not until years later did I begin to understand something of the pain I had caused them, and we were able to talk it through together and begin to heal the hurt. True, the summer camp had been a significant time in my Christian walk, a time of new insight and understanding, a time at which I began to see God not as distant but as a loving and personal heavenly Father – but it was nonetheless one of many steps in an ongoing and deepening relationship with God.

Calm before the storm

My new-found enthusiasm did not stop at home. I wanted to tell my friends at school about Jesus, so I wore a little badge on my school jumper which proclaimed 'Jesus Saves', hoping people would want to find out more and ask me. Actually, it brought me mockery and ridicule, which somewhat dampened my enthusiasm. Christians were very few and far between in my school, so it was quite a lonely time.

University was different. There were over one hundred students in the Christian Union, at least half of whom were eligible young men! To a shy, somewhat naive small-town girl, it was all a bit overwhelming! After the first fairly sheltered and comfortable eighteen years of my life, new experiences and new challenges were in abundance.

In the small coastal town in Scotland in which I had been brought up the only non-white faces I had seen were those of the family which ran the local Chinese restaurant. I had no clue about life in the outside world. So it came as quite a shock to me as I became aware for the first time of some of the injustices and inequalities in the world. I did not understand the details or the reasons, but I had a deep sense of discomfort and unease at the poverty of the Two-Thirds world. When Willy Brandt's *North-South Report* was published I joined a small group of students and lecturers to lobby our local MP. Not daring to ask any questions for fear that I would not understand the answers, I nonetheless had a gut feeling that life for so many in the world was just not fair, and that somebody somewhere should be doing something about it!

Gradually it began to dawn on me that I could not pass the buck forever, and just perhaps I ought to be looking at the possibility of doing something myself. Was this my 'call' into 'mission work'? I did not know what could be considered a call, or even what I understood by mission work. There were certainly no flashing lights, no thundering voice (not even a still, small one), no chapter and verse to point to. I simply saw something of the needs around the world, read in the Gospels of Jesus's compassion and care for the poor and oppressed, and began to realise that to take my faith seriously would mean responding to these challenges. It was another step on this journey of a growing relationship with God.

But where to go, and what to do? Was the desire to go to Africa simply romantic idealism? Having never been out of Europe, and having an intense dislike of spiders, could I honestly expect to survive more than a couple of days in a tropical country? The only way to find out surely was to test the waters, so I began investigating short-term postgraduate options. Confusion set in, however, when a short-term teaching opportunity in Africa fell through at the last minute.

Now what? A timely conversation with Tear Fund's Scottish co-ordinator a few weeks later inspired me to embark on post-graduate professional training – and thus it was that I went to London to begin my nursing career.

In terms of gaining a professional qualification which would be useful in the Two-Thirds world, I had opted for nursing on the grounds that it would mean fewer years of study than medicine. However, as I entered my *eighth* year in London, having completed both nursing and midwifery training, as well as gaining some staffing experience in both, I was beginning to wonder if I would *ever* make it to Africa!

My enthusiasm had been growing after a very short-term placement in Rwanda before beginning the midwifery training. To my relief I had found I could cope with the spiders and the heat, so what was there now to hold me back? I had experienced the warmth of hospitality and welcome, the amazing generosity in the face of poverty, and I longed to share in it more. But I had also seen the poor conditions, the lack of resources and the desperate needs, and felt, albeit somewhat naively, that I had something to offer. (The reality, as so many before me had discovered and I was to learn later, was that my contributions to their lives were tiny in comparison with the vast richness of experience I received from them.)

It was not an easy decision to make, though. There were several other pulls in different directions, and many options to consider. What would it mean to my career prospects? How would my parents cope? Was I saying goodbye to marriage possibilities? A well-meaning friend had suggested I stay at home and find myself a husband first, adding the caution, 'You'll be too late otherwise!' And she was probably right. After all, spending four years in a remote village of French-speaking Africa was not the most likely scenario for a single girl turning thirty to meet her lifelong partner. But then, surely if God wanted me to be married, he would be quite capable of matching me up with someone, however unlikely the circumstances. So also he could take care of my family and my future career prospects. If he wanted me to go, nothing should hold me back.

So . . . another decision on my journey with God. Again, no visions or dreams, no passage from Scripture, but instead a mixture of 'chance' conversations and opportunities, drawing on the relevance of past experience and studies, together with excitement and enthusiasm, all combined to convince me that a community health post in Gahini, Rwanda, was the next step in God's plan for my life.

So was I to be a missionary? To be honest, I felt uncomfortable with the term. Why should I be any different from the Christians who stayed at home? As far as I was concerned, I was going to do a professional job of work to the best of my ability, and seek to live out a faithful Christian life, albeit in a country and culture somewhat different to my own. If that was being a missionary, then I was a missionary. But if I was a missionary, then surely so also were all Christians who were seeking to live and witness faithfully to God in whatever circumstances – be it Gahini or Glasgow.

These middle years were years of growing and deepening in my relationship with God. On the whole they were fairly comfortable and safe, with no major incidents to rock the boat or cause me to question. Of course, there were times of hurt and disappointment, various changes of direction, broken relationships and periods of doubt. But God was always the thread of continuity running throughout, giving a purpose to push on for. Perhaps he was building a foundation in my life during these calmer waters, in order to prepare me for the hurricane-force storms that were soon to batter my life and my faith into tiny pieces.

'Why?' or 'what next?'

Over the next few years, Rwanda began to feel as much like home to me as Scotland. It was a fantastic place to live – a place of breathtaking physical beauty, with its rolling fertile hills and luscious green countryside. I quickly grew to appreciate the reserved but warm natures of my local friends and colleagues.

My job as co-ordinator of the Gahini Community Health Project brought me into a close working relationship and friendship with my immediate Rwandan colleague, Anatolie – a young wife with two bright little daughters. Together we were responsible for the training and supervision of some fifty community health workers, and our work with them gave us the privilege of contact with some of the poorest families living in the surrounding hills.

Our focus was largely preventative, and often involved home visiting among the families with particular difficulties. Anatolie was extremely good at building relationships and discussing health issues with them – the need for vaccinations against the killer diseases, prevention of recurrent malaria, treatment for dehydration through diarrhoea and worms, family planning, and so on. It was much harder for me to contribute anything very meaningful, struggling as I was not only with language barriers, but also with cultural barriers. How could I as a Westerner even begin to understand some of the pressures and hardships these families faced?

Living with a Rwandan family had helped enormously in giving me a feel of life from the inside and I was very grateful for Etienne and Emeralde's courage in agreeing to host me for my first six weeks in the country. They included me in their family – 'our sixth child', they used to tell people – little knowing that three years later their parental role would require them to give me away . . .

Negotiations for a wedding in Rwanda would normally take months, if not years, as representatives of the two families iron out the details of the agreement. As part of the gifts given by the groom's family to the bride's family, cattle usually play a key role. The higher the education of the bride, the more cattle will be asked for. Fortunately for Charles Bilinda, the standard exchange in the area in which we lived was one cow, regardless of the quality of the bride. I reckon he got a real bargain there!!

Charles was ordained as a pastor in the Episcopal Church of Rwanda, but his previous training was in teaching, and when we met he was working as an English teacher in the local church secondary school. Developing a relationship and coming to a decision to marry was far from easy, but we both were convinced it was the way ahead for us.

As well as a church wedding, part of the marriage celebrations took place in the home of Etienne and Emeralde, as the 'parents' of the bride. It was a vibrant, colourful affair, full of excitement. For several hours in Etienne's front yard we were entertained by an amazing variety of choirs, dancers and speeches, fed with chunks of beef and cooked bananas washed down with bottles of Fanta. A couple of weeks later my family returned to Scotland (leaving the cow with Etienne and Emeralde!) and life began to return to some degree of normality.

But normality did not last for long. Over the next year the political tensions in the country were rising and security deteriorated. Violent incidents were on the increase, and with the variety of conflicting explanations and rumours it was often impossible to tell who was to blame. Tensions were rising for Charles and me on the personal front also, as malicious rumours began to be spread about our private lives, and again it was impossible to know who to believe. Trust was breaking down on all levels around and between us. It was a horribly stressful situation to be caught up in, and I knew I needed a break.

Just a few days later, in the middle of a short holiday in neighbouring Kenya with my sister Sue, the Presidents of Rwanda and Burundi were killed, and the atrocities began. Growing increasingly desperate, I tried every means to get Charles out of the country, but it was all in vain. I was very strongly advised not to attempt to get back in myself – it would have been virtually impossible anyway – so there was nothing else to do but go back to the UK and wait.

News of friends and colleagues began to filter through – dear Anatolie and her husband murdered, my 'parents' and their family fled to Tanzania and struggling for survival with 300,000 others in refugee camps – but no news of Charles. The waiting was unbearable.

Initially I was convinced that through the power of prayer God would keep him safe, and yet the wider situation in the country seemed to belie such faith. Some ten thousand people were being slaughtered *every day*. It was beyond belief. What on earth was happening to the country which had become my home? How could I find anything sensible to say and maintain my composure before the media and growing opportunities for public speaking, when I was confused and crumbling inside?

Over these months my life was a strange fluctuation between deep distress, anguish and despair, and yet times of equally deep peace, restoring the calm and giving just enough strength to live another day. Deep down I was angry at God, yet was unable fully to vent my anger on him – how could I bite the hand that fed me? He was the only hope I had left, and despite the increasing rumours to the contrary, I was still holding out hope that he would protect Charles.

Six months later the full reality hit with a devastating blow. My first return trip to Rwanda brought me face to face with the fact that I was now a widow. There was no hope left. Charles had been taken by the military, and was assumed to have been shot. But despite the horror of this news, there was no space for me to grieve. Everywhere I went, every single person I met had been through their own hell and each was desperate to talk about it. And every place I went to bore the marks of the genocide – shallow mass graves littered with remnants of clothing and human bones, hauntingly empty houses, scrub growing over the rubble where once stood someone's home. The whole experience sickened me to the core. It was beyond belief. I was numb.

Why? Why had God not intervened? Why did he fail us? Now I was angry. There was no longer anything at stake, nothing to hold back for. Now I could vent all that had been building up inside over the past six months. If God could not take it, he was not worth following, I told myself.

And yet there was another side. In the midst of such devastation there was courage, hope and compassion. I spent a morning with Marion, a dear elderly friend who, along with her husband, had been a great support to Charles and me as we adjusted in our cross-cultural marriage. (One of their sons had married a Belgian lady.) She recounted to me the events that had led up to the death of her own husband, son and daughter-in-law, and other family members. Some forty relatives had been murdered, she calculated, and her home in Gahini destroyed. And yet, as she shared her experiences with me over several hours, I was struck by the total absence of any bitterness or resentment. No desire for revenge, no blaming God. Instead she was thanking God for the opportunities he was giving her to work among the war widows, seeking to bring them comfort and hope as she had experienced it herself. The contrast of this serenity and hope against the backdrop of horror was too deep for words.

I also spent some days in the refugee camp visiting Etienne and Emeralde and many others. Their tragedy had been, and still was, *so* much worse than mine, yet I picked up no anger or questioning from their lips either. Instead there was gratitude. Gratitude! After all that had happened to them, how could they be grateful? But they were. After all, they told me, they were still alive, they had stayed together as a family, they were being provided with some food and shelter by the aid agencies, and they even had jobs in the NGO (Non-governmental organisation) hospitals. In the midst of the devastation, there was joy and laughter. They were reaching out to others around – the poor, widows, orphans, the sick – and sharing their meagre resources and their plentiful love.

These attitudes challenged me profoundly. Over the previous few months I had read in a new light of several characters in the Bible who had suffered through no fault of their own, and who questioned or blamed God. There was Jeremiah, Job, some of the psalmists and various others. This had come as a huge relief to me. Not only had I felt I had no option but to vent my feelings on God, but I had discovered that it was actually OK to do so! After so many years of being 'polite' towards God, this was quite a revelation.

But now I was being challenged to take this further. My Rwandan friends were not angry, and nor could I remain angry with God for ever. How was I to come to terms with an experience of life which did not match up to my expectations and hopes – even to my prayers? I wondered if the apostle Paul struggled with these same questions? After all, he seemed to be pretty uncomfortable with his 'thorn' and gives us only the summary of a wrestling match he had with God over it (2 Corinthians 12:8). Yet through his struggling he came to a point of acceptance, seeing the bigger picture. Jesus too clearly agonised before his Father over the suffering that lay ahead of him, pleading with him to take it away if it were possible. Yet he then came to a position of willingness to accept: 'Not as I will, but as you will' (Matthew 26:39).

There is a mystery in suffering which cannot be understood. On one level, of course, it can be explained. We live in a fallen world where the majority of people have chosen to turn their backs on God and ignore his commands. We all have to bear the consequences of that, even if we personally are seeking to follow God. On that level it makes more sense to believe in God (and in Satan) than not to believe in him.

But on another level, I cannot understand why. Why were some protected miraculously and not others? Why do some wars stop before they get to this degree of devastation and not others?

Why are some healed and others continue in pain? There are no easy answers. There is no clever prayer formula which, once we have found it, will bring the desired answer to all our prayers. God's character and his ways cannot be brought down to our limited understanding. Some things are too mysterious.

Previously I had thought that, in simple terms, if we are reasonably faithful to God and try to be obedient, then he will bring blessing. But if we are disobedient then we will be punished and suffering will result. Life, however, as I came to understand it, is not so simple. Indeed, had I read my Bible more carefully, I would have understood this long ago, for many others had questioned such theology long before me (for example, see Jeremiah 12:1; Job 21:7-15; Psalm 73:3-12; 2 Corinthians 1:8-11).

Instead of carefully worked out and logical reasons, I found God's people trying to come to terms with their painful situations and, dare I say it, seeking to turn their tragedies into something positive: perhaps it was in terms of an awareness of the privilege of sharing in the sufferings of Christ (1 Peter 4:12-13); or of a deepening dependency on God (2 Corinthians 5:8); perhaps it was in finding ways of blessing others through their misfortunes (Joseph in Genesis 50:20; Paul in 2 Corinthians 1:3-6). In a variety of ways they were moving on from the immediate 'why' questions.

The situations which I read about in the Bible I could see matched in the lives of my Rwandan friends. Marion was not sitting around asking why, and feeling sorry for herself. No. Her attitude was different, and therefore her actions were too. She was looking out of herself, responding to the needs of others around her by bringing encouragement and comfort. So also were Etienne and Emeralde in the camps, as well as countless others, known and unknown.

What about me? What was to be *my* attitude? How was *I* to live now? Even if I didn't have all the answers, did I know enough of God to leave the unanswered questions with him, and get on with living for him? Could he possibly use these horrific experiences to bring some good for others? Could I move from the 'Why?' to the 'What next?'

As I write this around five years after the genocide in Rwanda, I am all too aware that the pain has not gone completely. Although life has moved on in remarkable and exciting ways, I have to accept that there is a brokenness inside me which will always remain. But this does not stop me from enjoying life to the full – in fact, in a strange way it enables me to appreciate life so much more.

Five years ago everything in my life was thrown totally up in the air: no stone left unturned, no question left unasked. The foundations of my life and my faith were shaken till it felt they would crumble into oblivion. Everything had been stripped away from me – my security, my identity, my husband and friends, my possessions, my future. I was left in my nakedness, face to face with God. There was no place for pat answers. Just stark reality. I came to the brink of giving up altogether but somehow, by God's grace, I pulled back.

Now I know I can continue with greater conviction than ever before, for in the space of two years God showed himself to me more intimately and more radically than throughout the previous thirty-plus years put together. Perhaps a bit like Job, whose questions and arguing brought him not answers but an overwhelming encounter with God, I dare to say that my ears had heard of him, but now my eyes have seen him (Job 42:5).

Just as there was nothing mediocre about living in Rwanda, but instead the extremes of human emotion and experience – of depths of loneliness yet heights of exhilaration, of intense frustration yet deep satisfaction, of crushing disappointment yet exciting fulfilment – so, in my experience, is the Christian life. Some of the paths I have travelled along I would most definitely not have chosen, and many times I wished I could have been left in my secure comfort zone. But I have no regrets, having seen the reality of God's faithfulness and care *through* the pain, not only in my own life, but also the lives of numerous others.

So what about my friend's question about giving up on God and Christianity? 'To whom shall we go?' Simon Peter asked. What more can I say than to echo Peter's response, that in Christ alone are 'the words of eternal life'? There is no better way, nothing and no one else that makes sense of the experience of life, brings comfort in pain, strength to persevere, and purpose to continue with life.

10

Hand to the Plough

David Pawson

I entered this world in 1930 with a head start in the Christian race, living proof that at least one 'Tuesday's child is full of grace' (a word I take to mean undeserved favour rather than irresistible force). Born a Geordie in Newcastle on Tyne, I inherited Scottish and Yorkshire blood, which may explain my temperament.

Mother's Sinclair clan had a crest with the motto: 'Commit thy work to God' and her tobacco-manufacturing family had Presbyterian, Brethren and Methodist connections. She fell in love with a lay preacher who began his sermon with the memorable line: 'Life is a long straight road full of twistings and turnings.' It was my father.

Professor Cecil Pawson, as many later knew him, came from Wakefield stock. The family crest included the Latin motto: '*Favente deo* (favoured by God)' and the surname means 'son of a peacock' (I'd rather have this bird as an ancestor than a monkey).

I was named 'John David' after my two grandfathers. One name was the same as Jesus's beloved disciple in the New Testament and the other means 'beloved of God' and belonged to the king in the Old Testament. I often wonder how far genes and names affect our lives.

Heredity and environment combined in my Methodist heritage. Father liked to claim a line of farmers and preachers back to John Pawson, one of Wesley's first colleagues. He himself was one of Methodism's most loyal and active supporters, rising to the highest position for a layman, Vice-President of Conference. For over forty years he devoted every Tuesday evening to a 'class-meeting' of men, every Saturday evening to counselling individuals and almost every Sunday to preaching (he kept a book listing names and addresses of 'decisions' or 'rededications' in response to his appeals, over twelve thousand of them).

Our home was the base for every well-known visiting preacher to Tyneside. The big three London Methodists – Leslie Weatherhead (who loved people), Will Sangster (who loved the Lord) and Donald, later Lord, Soper (who loved an argument); people from other denominations – Martin Lloyd-Jones, James Stewart, Alan Redpath; international figures like the Japanese Toyohiko Kagawa and the German Martin Niemöller. Sadly, I was too young to appreciate this galaxy of spiritual giants, but who knows what subconscious seeds were planted by meeting these 'Preachers out of the Pulpit' (the title of a movie film made by my mother, a keen photographer)?

The cliché 'brought up in a godly home' certainly applied in my case. Sunday was a case in point. Bicycles, cameras and toys were put away (I never understood why). Morning was spent in church (sitting through the sermon). Family prayers followed lunch (taking the edge off the pleasure of roast beef and Yorkshire pudding). Afternoon was filled with Sunday school (my teacher is now in his nineties and still riding his racing cycle). Evening was spent at home when my sisters (both later married Methodist ministers and both died of cancer, one at thirty-six and the other at sixty-nine) and I took it in turns to 'lead' a service, preaching from the back of a reversed armchair. On one occasion I had read the parable of the labourers in the vineyard, retold it, explained it, and was about to review it, when my older sister wearily remarked: 'Isn't that vineyard full yet?' Matthew 20 is still one of my favourite sermons.

With such a background many would think it virtually inevitable that I would follow in my forebears' footsteps. Indeed, I once made a rather feeble attempt to do so. Before I was even a teenager, World War 2 made me an 'evacuee', sent away from home to a school billeted in a Windermere hotel. Urged on by letters from home, I tried to start a 'Christian club', but it quickly fizzled out. Incidentally, severe bullying, which led to expulsions, taught me to keep a low profile, which may explain why I have remained a rather 'private' person, in spite of my public reputation. The truth was that I had accepted parental convictions and commitments as a matter of course, so my 'faith' was second-hand. I had yet to learn that God has no grandsons.

As the threat of bombing subsided, I returned home. Holidays were spent on the superb Northumbrian coast, where trips in old Model 'A' Ford cars through the tidal shallows to Lindisfarne, 'Holy Island', acquainted me with Celtic saints Aidan and Cuthbert. I cannot quantify the influence of this attractive stream of Christianity, but I know it became part of me, especially years later when I stayed on Columba's island of Iona, in the community rebuilding the ancient abbey under George MacLeod's leadership.

The real test of my faith came when I left home for the second time at the age of sixteen, determined to pursue my ambition to be a farmer. Compared to the interest and independence of a life close to nature, careers in commercial, industrial, technical, legal, medical and especially ecclesiastical spheres held no appeal for me whatever. My first job exposed me to the dreadful winter of 1947, the snow cutting us off for weeks at a time. Nor was I put off by rising at 4 a.m. to milk ninety cows.

But my sheltered upbringing was over. The language and lifestyle of 'earthy' colleagues, male and female, awakened me to the real world in which most live. At first I kept up church attendance, though it involved the 'sin' of cycling. I often fell asleep during the sermon, since cows don't observe sabbaths. But my heart was not in it and, inevitably, attendance declined. Village-hall dances were much more interesting at that age. Not that I strayed far from the straight and narrow. Habits die hard. There was never a conscious rebellion against my background. It was simply slipping away. My state was somewhere between the prodigal son and his elder brother.

I have sometimes wished I had been a criminal or a cannibal. Then I would have a much more exciting and impressive testimony. Where sin has been more sensational, salvation is more spectacular. This tempts us to draw a sharper contrast between pre- and post-conversion lives than is the case. And I want to be truthful in this account. I have had to realise two important truths about the sin from which we need to be saved:

The first is that sin is not necessarily doing what is bad in other people's eyes, but doing what is wrong in God's eyes, which can be quite different. It can even be simply doing what is right in our own eyes, doing our own thing (which I was doing), ignoring God's directions for life, both general and particular.

The second is that we need to be saved from future as well as past sin. Looking back, the direction of my drifting course would have taken me far down the broad way, had it continued. From what was already happening, I now know what a wasted and even wicked life could have followed, had Jesus himself not stepped in to prevent it. I am more conscious of having been rescued from what the future would have been than from what the past was. For those who find redemption earlier rather than later, gratitude springs from imagination as well as memory and the absence of regret over wasted years or remorse over damage to one's self and others is a matter for praise. At any rate, I was one of the early ones.

It happened on 9 September 1947. I was invited to a family 'holiday' in a country house in Kent called Hildenborough Hall. An evangelist called Tom Rees (husband to my cousin Jean and father to Justyn Rees and Jennifer Rees Larcombe) used it as a conference centre for young people and a base for rallies in his 'little mission hall in Kensington' (the Royal Albert Hall). The leaders included two decorated Battle of Britain pilots but I encountered other 'heroes' among the guests – youngsters of my own age for whom their faith was so real and precious that they were willing to suffer verbal and even physical abuse for it, at home or at work. Clearly, they had 'something' I didn't have; and it didn't take long to realise it was Someone.

By the last evening my mind was clear, my heart was focussed and my will was ready. Around 8.45 p.m. (the very time when John Wesley 'felt his heart strangely warmed') I jumped to my feet and 'confessed with my mouth'. To this day I have no recollection of what I said, but it was what was happening inside me that mattered. Quite simply I knew for certain that Jesus was for real and for me. Life could never be the same again.

It wasn't so much a 'decision' as a surrender – to all that the Lord had already done for me and given to me, without my realising it. But now I knew who to thank and how to show it. I was not 'counselled', perhaps because it was thought it was not needed in my circumstances. In retrospect, I wish I had been told about being baptised in water and 'receiving' the Spirit. It was going to take another seventeen years to complete my initiation into the full life of the kingdom. Maybe early starters are slow runners!

But there had been a real change. Returning to the farm, I sang to the cows as I milked them (years later, an article in *Farmers' Weekly* claimed that piped music in the cowshed improved milk yield – I could have held the patent). Soon I was taking a B.Sc. in agriculture, which included studying a number of sciences. This introduced me to some of the tensions with Scripture, particularly in the lectures on evolution (by a Christian professor). I am glad that I had to wrestle with these so quickly; it has helped when asked to speak in schools and colleges. I learned to think with clarity and integrity.

I had begun to 'preach', though not in churches at first. With a growing team of young Christians, I found myself speaking to cinema queues, in pubs and clubs, on promenades and beaches – in fact, anywhere people were gathered and would listen. The first time in a real pulpit was due to the wiles of a converted bookmaker, who invited me to accompany him to a Durham chapel one Sunday evening and on the bus journey there told me I was to preach. I got through my entire theology in seven minutes flat, a feat of which I have been utterly incapable ever since.

For some reason I was far more nervous facing believers than unbelievers. Diarrhoea before, Pharaoh's plague of frogs in my throat during (draining many pulpit glasses of water, most of which were an interesting study in pond life) and mental agonies after, remembering what I had or hadn't said – probably reinforcing my dependence on the Lord and determination to do better.

I was heading for a real conflict of interest. I now wanted to be a farmer and a preacher. Could it be both? Must it be either? If so, which? I had then, and still have today, a simple approach to divine guidance. The Lord is my boss. I don't have to try and read his mind. It is his responsibility to tell me what he wants me to do or say or where he wants me to go. I have promised him that if he tells me clearly I will be obedient. Of course, I now know what consequences there can be to such an arrangement, both pleasant and painful. But it works.

So here I was, having asked which it was to be. Over coffee that morning a fellow-student remarked: 'You'll finish up in a pulpit, not behind a plough.' I recall thinking that wasn't clear enough! Leaving him I walked down the street, only to bump into a retired minister I had not seen for years. His first words were: 'David, why aren't you in the ministry?' That was clear enough. Out of the mouth of two witnesses . . .

My course was set, even if it could not be immediately followed. Only when the decision was taken did I discover that my father had already arranged for me to rent a small farm when I reached the age of twenty-one. But Jesus had warned his followers that putting a hand to the plough and looking back with regret would render them unfit for his kingdom. The farm had to go. My hand was on another kind of plough now, 'rightly dividing the word of truth' (2 Timothy 2:15, the verb is literally 'straight-cutting').

Since my church membership, background and links were all Methodist, that seemed the appropriate 'ministry' to consider. I have since discovered that the Head of the Church doesn't think denominationally and calls us to serve his body, opening doors into whatever part of it we can be most effective in for him – and which can change, as I was to find out.

After completing my degree I knocked on the Methodist door, but their process of selection could not be finalised for twelve months. I offered this year to them for service 'anywhere in the United Kingdom' – so they sent me to the Shetland Isles (which until then, I thought were in a 'box' in the Firth of Forth off Edinburgh, according to my school atlas). I was to be 'lay pastor' to five churches. This was before the oil boom, when crofters and fishermen struggled to survive, the young left to get jobs in the south and poor nutrition took its toll. By the time I left these homely and hardy people, they had taught me far more than I ever taught them. Their simple faith was engraved on my memory, along with the treeless hills, towering cliffs, wheeling birds, howling gales, endless winters and 'pretty dancers' (Northern Lights, or aurora borealis).

The transition to sophisticated Cambridge was in marked contrast. My faith in God never faltered, but my faith in his Word certainly did. We read the Bible with a pair of scissors, cutting it up and even cutting things out. Our tutors were already big names in the scholars' world. C. H. Dodd was chairing the translation of the New English Bible. John A. T. Robinson was later famous (infamous?) for his disturbing book: *Honest to God*, but I have to say that his lectures on Paul's letter to the Romans were inspiring, and I was relieved when he returned to his confidence in the New Testament after leaving his episcopal office.

I managed to emerge with my 'evangelical' convictions intact, if only just. Though I have joked about 'emptying the churches by degrees', I am not anti-theological. The exposure to critical analysis of the Bible has made me think through what I believe and in the long run made me more sure than ever that the truths revealed in Scripture are utterly reliable. My preaching has been criticised for being too definite, even dogmatic. But it is not that I think I have the truth. It is the truth that has me. In Bunyan's *Pilgrim's Progress*, the character I most identify with is Mr Valiant-for-truth.

But I had not yet found my life's vocation, which I would not do until my roots in Methodism had been loosened and then pulled up altogether. For a year I served a 'circuit' of churches in the Thames Valley, lodging with two Spiritualist spinsters (neither they nor I changed our views). Then I was sent to the South Yorkshire coalfields as an evangelist, with a caravan to live in and a mobile cinema van to pull it. Though the results were encouraging, I came to the (correct) conclusion that I am not an evangelist (and still take occasional 'crusades' to prove it). However, in one village I met a doctor's secretary in a mobile x-ray unit, combating tuberculosis. Her first conversation with me was about believers' baptism; her own doubts about 'christening' echoed my own and were to prove prophetic (she would be the first person I ever immersed). We soon found we had much more in common and got engaged. That was the second best decision I ever made, as those who know her would confirm. We now have a son and two daughters, one of whom is already in heaven with Jesus, having contracted leukaemia a few years ago.

We had expected a long engagement, since I had been interviewed and selected to be a chaplain in the Royal Air Force (O.D. = other denominations, i.e. everyone other than RC = Roman Catholic, or C/E = Church of England). But my first posting was to a station with an empty 'married quarter' and we got it on the same morning as a hastily arranged marriage.

Church life in the forces was very different, like changing from a lifeboat (women and children first) to a battleship (men only), though my fellow-officers would not have appreciated such a naval metaphor! My style simply had to change when preaching to hundreds of men in a hut or praying before thousands on a parade-ground. Men want it 'straight from the shoulder' even if they disagree; and this has left me with a legacy of plain speaking which is not always appreciated in other situations! There were two other developments which were to change my ministry quite radically.

My 'old' sermons, prepared in and for civvy street congregations, were clearly not suitable for men in uniform, especially in compulsory parade services. I had to find another way to make God real and relevant. On an impulse (in hindsight a prompting of the Spirit) I announced a series of talks covering the whole Bible ('from Generation to Revolution'). The results surprised all of us. This was big enough for the men to get their teeth into, a vision of history that gave point to individual lives, an understanding of the whole purpose of God that would motivate a change in lifestyle.

I had found my life's calling, without even guessing what it would lead to. I abandoned 'text' preaching (one verse a sermon) and much 'topic' preaching (many verses from all over the place) and devoted myself to 'expository' preaching (usually a chapter at a time, working through whole books at a time). Little did I dream that this shift would one day give me a worldwide platform, reaching many thousands of people and changing their lives.

Meanwhile, the Bible became a new book. Every 'text' had to take its meaning from the context and could no longer be used as a pretext for what I wanted to say. God now had his say. The new light breaking out from his Word was as exciting for me as it was to the growing number of servicemen listening (it is a joy to meet them today and find the effects were lasting).

But my own understanding was changing, too. Seeing the Bible whole can radically alter the meaning of its parts. All the biblical data had to be taken into account, making for better balance. Passages hitherto ignored, either consciously or unconsciously, now demanded attention. This led to the other major development which was to affect my whole future.

I had overlooked the thirty-one passages dealing with baptism but now had to face up to them. Perhaps I was also influenced by the cost faced by converts after being baptised in the country of my overseas posting. Suffice it to say that I became convinced that immersion of repenting believers was the New Testament norm – for now as well as then, for me as well as others. I could not in conscience christen any more babies, including our own children. I managed to avoid doing so for the rest of my S.S.C. (Short Service Commission; I was now a Squadron Leader), but faced a crisis on 'demobilisation'.

I told the Methodist authorities about my new conviction. I was even offered the services of a full-time deaconess to do the christenings if I'd stay. But the Conference overruled and I was packed off to Lancashire (Eliza Street, Ramsbottom!) to see if I thought differently in a 'normal' church setting. It was soon obvious that I could never fit the Methodist system again, not least because my understanding of the Bible was now at variance with the views of so many of the other preachers sharing the same pulpits.

I must do the right thing and resign. I remember telling my wife that it would mean losing job, home and pension in one fell swoop. Her immediate reply was: 'I want to be married to a man who obeys God.' Blessed is the man with such a partner. We lost everything and we lost nothing. Within days we were living in a brand-new home and I was pastor of Gold Hill Baptist Church in Buckinghamshire, where we were to spend seven wonderful years, adapting to a rural village rapidly becoming part of the commuter belt around London.

This move marked the full and final release into my life's work, though I did not realise it at the time. On the one hand, I was free from family tradition, reputation and expectation. I was now moving in circles where the name 'Pawson' was hardly known, so I could be myself. On the other hand, I now had a regular pulpit, giving me the opportunity of consecutive and therefore consistent teaching in a pastoral setting. Both here and later at the Millmead Centre in Guildford, I proved that this makes for growth in quantity and quality, though neither was simply a 'preaching centre'. I found personal counselling, small groups and other aspects of leading a fellowship just as rewarding. Even the buildings reflected 'the work of my hands', both in design and construction (I still draw plans for church centres, my best probably being at Coton Green, Tamworth).

Audiotapes of my Bible teaching, originally made for the sick and housebound, began to circulate more widely, eventually reaching over one hundred countries, in all continents, including Antarctica. I began to be invited to speak at conferences and conventions, acquiring a reputation as a 'sound evangelical'. Then I had to go and spoil it all, by becoming a 'charismatic'.

I had never been comfortable preaching about the Holy Spirit. It was a relief to get through Whit Sunday and get back to the gospel! But systematic exposition forced me to face what both Jesus and his cousin John repeatedly referred to as being 'baptised in Holy Spirit'. I decided to preach a series of twenty sermons, covering every mention of the Spirit in the Bible. Halfway through this, when praying for the healing of a deacon, I was 'filled' to overflowing, pouring out a new language. The deacon was healed and changed from being a self-appointed leader of the opposition (there seems to be one in every church!) to one of my best friends and closest colleagues. The Sunday after this happened a carpenter in the congregation said to me: 'What's happened to you? You know what you're talking about now.'

I see this as the completion of my initiation into New Testament Christianity. But back in the 1960s, such an experience was far from common outside Pentecostal circles and only just beginning to appear in older denominations. However, I was convinced from Scripture of its validity, so preached it, even though this began to close many of the doors that had opened.

Which brings me to another aspect of my pilgrimage, one which is often omitted from testimonies. Jesus said following him would mean 'big trouble'. Holiness here and happiness hereafter is his programme. How often we want to reverse it. But I want to be honest. There has been a cost, which would have been harder to bear without a supportive wife and a few faithful friends.

I had made a solemn promise to the Lord that whatever I clearly found in Scripture I would teach others, whether it fitted in with what they or I believed or not. I would be more afraid of grieving the Lord than upsetting people (I've certainly managed the latter and am regularly introduced as 'no stranger to controversy').

It is not that I think myself infallible. I study the views of others, particularly those I know would differ from me. I have three tons of books, according to the removal firm that brought our goods here, filling two rooms and the garden shed in which I am writing. So I sit at the feet of teachers from all over the world and from all ages. But after all that I come to my own conclusion and preach that with all my heart and mind.

But this has led me to a growing number of minority views in the contemporary climate. Spirit baptism and the belief that Israel is still God's covenant people were among the first, along with believers' baptism. Classic (as distinct from dispensational) premillennialism and hell as everlasting torment (as against annihilationism) soon followed. Espousal of male leadership and the possibility of losing salvation probably isolated me more than other stances. And I am currently working on the teaching of Jesus that remarriage after divorce is adultery, and on the 'deGreecing' of the church (Augustine's neo-Platonism having corrupted the theology of Catholics and Protestants alike, separating the spiritual and the physical, the sacred and the secular, the eternal and the temporal, heaven and earth in an unbiblical way). Publicising these 'burdens' by writing books has not increased my popularity. If ever I write a full autobiography, which I have no desire to, I am tempted to call it: 'How to lose friends and influence people'.

There has been opposition, not easy to bear when it comes from fellow-believers, especially in the form of isolation. But the most painful aspect is the number of those who privately agree with what I am teaching but are afraid to say so publicly. There have been frequent rumours of my death for the last twenty years, but I tell those who enquire or offer my wife condolences that it's all wishful thinking. Slanderous lies used to hurt until the Lord one day said to me: 'The worst they can say about you is not as bad as the truth and I still love and use you.' My wife roared with laughter at that, knowing me as she does and it cured me of having any concern for my reputation.

As fast as one door closed, another opened. Soon I was following my tapes overseas with increasing regularity. It was beginning to be impossible to combine this with looking after a church with five congregations and forty-five house cells. A very clear prophetic word led the elders to release me and devote my whole time to itinerant ministry here and overseas, with particular emphasis on men and church leaders. Videos have opened more doors (it has recently taken five years to put the whole Bible into this format). Radio and the Internet are now opening up.

And I've entered my seventieth year on planet earth while writing this. But that's not the beginning of the end, just the end of the beginning. I've asked the Lord if I can serve him till I'm in the 'four score' bracket, but he hasn't replied yet. Even that lifespan would only be a foretaste of the goodness and mercy that have dogged my footsteps thus far (as an ex-shepherd, I call them the Lord's sheepdogs).

I am dying (literally and metaphorically) to put on my new immortal body (half the age of this old one if it's going to be 'like his glorious body'). I look forward to returning with Christ (if I die first, which begins to look possible) and reigning with him over this old world for the best 'millennium' ever, the devil at last banished from the scene. Then on into a recycled universe, life in the perfect garden city and 'God-with-us' on earth, as at the beginning. What a prospect!

It is a well-worn cliché but still true: the best is yet to be. And all because of that day over fifty years ago. Surely the best decision I ever made. But 'best' for whom? For myself? For other people? For God himself? Looking back, my 'conversion' was certainly the best thing that ever happened to me. I don't think I could have had a more interesting, full or varied life. I just think of all the people I have known, right across the social spectrum, from heads of state to 'lifers' in prison, from gypsies to powerful and wealthy businessmen. In one day I have gone from the palatial mansion of an ambassador to a longhouse in the jungle, full of people and animals but empty of furniture. Who says Christians live narrow lives? Usually those locked in their own little set. I have ministered to white (pink) and black (brown) congregations (we are all coloured and the Lord is colour-blind). And perhaps my most enriching contacts have been with God's chosen people, the Jews, both in their own land and around the world. I have stayed in Palestinian Arab homes as well, astonished to find some of them sharing my faith in God's future purpose for Israel.

I love flying. My very first venture into the air was in the first Missionary Aviation Fellowship plane, with the founding men (I am still in touch with them) – just three months after I became a Christian. Recently I have flown in the cockpits of a jumbo to Hong Kong and an Airbus around Europe, courtesy of Christian pilots, as well as in small private planes around New Zealand and Australia.

I have discovered that the Lord is interested in every part of our lives, even our hobbies. When I decided to build a model railway some years ago, my wife thought I'd entered my second childhood (she was probably right; she usually is). But very shortly after, a complete stranger at a conference pushed a cheque into my hand with: 'The Lord has told me to give you this for your new hobby, whatever it is.' I was more excited about the Giver behind the gift than the gift itself.

It has been a wonderful life (still is) and I would not change places with anyone. Had the decisions been left to me, life could have been a mess, full of regrets at the end and with little to show for it.

I believe it has been 'best' for others, too. Deep down, all of us want to help as many others as possible. Of course, only eternity will reveal how much good influence we have had. But God has graciously encouraged me by my seeing or hearing the fruit of my ministry in the lives of many individuals – from the little boy asking me to pray that the warts on his fingers would go (which they did), to telling Mrs Thatcher she would become Prime Minister (which she did, though I hasten to add that I also 'predicted' Bob Hawke for Australia, lest you think the Lord is politically partial). It is humbling to know how many have come to faith or to more mature grasp of the faith through tapes, videos or books. I could not have asked for more opportunities to serve others, though I know I could have served them better. Which brings me to the most delicate questions of all: Has it been 'best' for God? What did he get out of all this?

Well, he did get a servant. Whether my service passes the test of his fire, which consumes hay and stubble but refines gold and silver, remains to be seen. He is clearly more interested in the quality than the quantity of our labours, whether they are of lasting value. The prophecy which released me to the last twenty years of travelling ministry ended with the words: '. . . and I want you to go out and so serve me that one day you will look into my face and say: "Lord, we did it." ' How I want that to happen.

But I have no difficulty in accepting Jesus's verdict that even when we have done our best, we are still unprofitable servants. Writing out this testimony (the first time I've done it) has reminded me of all that he has done for me and poured into me. The return on his investment is minute by comparison. That's not mock modesty, just a simple fact.

And the Heavenly Father did get another son for his growing family – which was his original hope when forming me in the womb, as it is for every human being. Again, the contrast between his love for me and mine for him is humbling, to say the least. I am more aware than anyone else of the disappointments and heartaches I must have caused him. But those are between me and him. Grace does not allow us to grovel. The prodigal was firmly reminded he was a son, not a servant.

And he hasn't finished with me yet. Nor has he any intention of doing so, asking only that I go on trusting and obeying him right to the end. That is my intention, having put my hand to the plough.

11

Glory and Grace

Julie Sheldon

The empty cigarette packet lay crumpled among the dead leaves. I stared at it for some time then started rolling bits of silver foil into balls to take aim at the box. The darkness and shelter of the rhododendron bushes seemed an appropriate place to be at that moment. I had experienced my first 'smoke' at the tender age of eight amidst the shrubs of my grandparents' Tunbridge Wells garden where I had disliked the choking experience, enjoyed the sense of being 'grown up and naughty', and yet was disgusted that people actually did this for pleasure. A few years later I found a safe haven in the undergrowth of the garden at Elmhurst Ballet School. It was at this school that I hoped to fulfil a burning ambition to become a ballerina and the garden again drew me to a secret rendezvous. This time I wasn't smoking but building a sort of 'shrine' to the god of ballet, hoping he might hear my cries and desires to be a better dancer. I so remember the stillness of the afternoon, the dusty part of the wood that wasn't 'out of bounds' and the sun streaming on to my little altar of wild flowers and acorn cups. The warm summer rays created a haze and the nearness of God was tangible to a young eleven-year-old heart, so much so that I made a vow at that point that if I didn't become a prima ballerina I should have to become a nun!

A perfect shot. At last the silver foil ball hit the target and my thoughts turned to why this time I was sitting alone in a rhododendron bush in the middle of Dorset! My sister Annie had quite literally dragged me off to a camp for girls. We had travelled down in the car with a friend called Peter who was as reluctant as me about the forthcoming week. The boys' camp was taking place a few miles away from ours, which seemed rather unnecessary and tantalising to a seventeen-year-old, and as Peter dropped us off we agreed that if it 'all became too much and heavy' we could at least try and meet up at a nearby pub! Our concern was well founded, or so we thought, because these camps were being organised and run by Christians with the aim that young people could learn about the Christian faith in a fun setting, with plenty of activities and time for talks, discussion and an opportunity to make new friends. I know that as I slunk out of Peter's car my heart was dead set against enjoying myself; I was only doing this because my sister really wanted me to come and wouldn't have come by herself. Along with my luggage, cigarettes and plenty of 'attitude' we were welcomed at the imposing front door of an enormous old school and ushered into the entrance hall by the allocated 'friend'. This 'friend' was of similar age to myself and helpfully told us she could direct and take us to the dormitory that would be home for a week. The twelve beds looked particularly uninviting in the darkness of the attic room, but I did notice a large fire door at the far end with a wonderful escape route and that suddenly led to some very appealing thoughts! Our beds had already been allocated and my sister was the other end of the row from me but I was nearer the fire escape!

I had been trying to run away from something, someone, inside for a while. After fifteen years of training, my ballet career was suddenly cut short by an accident. While rehearsing one day at the Royal Ballet School in London my boy partner's hands had slipped as we were practising a lift, and I had fallen to the floor, fracturing my spine. Apart from the visible physical pain it had caused, the invisible emotional turmoil had not been wrapped in plaster of Paris to be given time to heal. The wounds were raw but I was trained to hide what was really going on inside; our ballet discipline taught that however we might be feeling, the pain of bleeding toes inside tight pointe shoes or the ache of overstrained muscles, the public would expect a first-class performance for after all they had paid 'good money' to come and watch us dance. The price for smiles, perfection and radiance cost a great deal in tears, fatigue and pain. This deep entrenched training ethos spilled out into everyday life. It was therefore making it difficult to fulfil my alternative vow to God to become a nun should this unthinkable situation occur of not reaching the heights of prima ballerina. The show must go on. The physical scars healed, the inward ones did not.

I was embarrassed, even a little ashamed, to think about God too much. Faith had played an important part in our family during my childhood and I was aware now, sitting smoking in the bushes, that God could hardly be pleased with my current lifestyle. London life, the theatre, the modelling and modern dance I became involved with after the Royal Ballet seemed a far cry from the lives the girls in our twelve-bedded dormitory were experiencing. Compared with the exciting 'adult' life I was enjoying in London this camp felt too restricting, the people too 'nice', so much so that when on the first morning there was a prayer meeting before breakfast I imagined I must be in a run of a new West End comedy! I felt as different from my fellow girls as if I had two heads. And yet, something got to me. Something stirred deep in the raw unhealed scars. No matter how rude or anti-social my behaviour might have seemed it was always met with acceptance and care. Even if I tried to shock with stories of flamboyant accounts of London life they still showed me the same love and kindness. Somehow the glittering theatre world began to seem hollow and pointless, just an illusion of happiness compared with the peace and joy this group of young people had found in God. Maybe it was time to come out of the rhodo-dendrons.

There was lots of singing and the house was full of music. As I ambled up from the garden towards the house a thought occurred and I couldn't get away from it, these girls *enjoyed* being Christians. This relationship with Jesus they talked about seemed to be real, exciting and lasting and I realised that over the past years I'd made an awful caricature of this man, used his name as a swear word, and written off Christians as boring, sad and rather missing out on the fun of life. How wrong I was. One evening a talk was given on the verse 'Here I am! I stand at the door and knock. If anyone hears my voice and opens the door, I will come in' (Rev. 3:20). The speaker accompanied her talk with a copy of the famous painting by Holman Hunt depicting Jesus standing knocking at a door without a door handle; the explanation being there was only one handle and that was on the *inside*, therefore it was up to *us* whether or not we opened the door to let Jesus into our lives. Our choice. Free will. Step of faith. The best decision you'll ever make. A strange quickening of my heart mixed with so many thoughts and fears. I knew this would mean surrendering all my hopes, ambitions and desires to him. Would I still be able to dance professionally? What did God think of success and fame? But what would my friends think if I stopped going to the wild parties and went to church instead? I could already hear their laughter.

The music and singing started up once more and this time the words stuck in my throat. Everything paled into insignificance as I faced this decision; this love that was being freely offered; the tenderness of the words falteringly left my lips:

> Turn your eyes upon Jesus,
> Look full in his wonderful face,
> And the things of earth will grow strangely dim
> In the light of his glory and grace.

I slipped quietly out of the room and went up to the fire escape balcony at the end of the dormitory. I gazed up into the clear starlit night. There seemed to be no one else in the world in that stillness, just God and me meeting at the very centre of creation. Nothing else mattered except that Jesus had loved me enough to die on the cross, and wanted to share his life with *me*. 'Yes, Lord', I whispered into the night, 'I open the door, please come in'. And just in case he hadn't heard I repeated it twenty times or more. Suddenly I was silent. All I could sense was the pounding of my heart and the enormity of the decision I had just made. Out of the heavens his love swept into my heart. A new feeling of excitement, wonder and reverence filled me as I realised, now without doubt, that Jesus *had* come through the door and into my life. For a long time I just stood on the balcony breathing in the peace and beauty of his presence. By the time I returned inside the other eleven were tucked up and asleep.

The next morning, instead of hiding and groaning under my bed covers while the girls got up, I was so surprised to find the feeling of the previous night had not left me, and an excitement and joy made me leap up to reach for the Bible helpfully left on my side locker. I couldn't wait to read it! Somehow, overnight, I seemed to understand that this wasn't just a boring old book any longer, but the Living Word of God. He was going to speak to me! I opened my Bible at the book of Proverbs and devoured page after page. It all seemed so relevant and up-to-date and perfectly attuned to my own situation. I felt a little apprehensive as to how I would break the news to my sister and actually tried to avoid her at breakfast, but in the end I didn't have to say anything. She took one look at my face and threw her arms around me with joy. Peter and I never did meet up in the pub but one look at his face on the return journey was enough to know that this had been a very special life-changing week for all of us.

Many years later while confined to a wheelchair, suffering from the neurological illness Dystonia, trying hard to endure the painful tremors and spasms that wracked my body, I recalled my sojourns in the undergrowth. This illness was like a spreading bramble, tearing and spoiling, contorting and strangling bit by bit, piece by piece, until I needed help with feeding, dressing and bathing. It was bewildering. Despite all the prayers, all the faith, all the apparent promises from God about healing, I was getting steadily worse. And yet after three years of increasing disability the sun filtered through. More and more people had this conviction that God had a far greater plan than just healing my body. In fact, we realised that God's healing *always* involves more than that. I had already seen that he wanted me to learn how to be honest with myself and those around me instead of hiding my feelings. I had a growing understanding that I was loved and accepted by God and by others – not for what I could achieve or the performance I could give, but for who I was. Now I was learning just how great and gracious God always is when he deals with us, that there is an extravagance in his love to us which overflows as blessing into other people's lives. The brambles were being cleared. The dead leaves burnt. A clearing was coming into view.

The extraordinary thing about illness is how quickly it robs you of things you love and take for granted. My ballerina body that I had so much control over now became an object of contortion and pain. I had no control of the twisting spasms and no performance to give the paying public. My husband and two lovely young daughters tried to adapt to a disabled wife and mother and we prayed. We asked God to make Mummy better. 'Every night I prayed for you, Mummy', wailed our then six-year-old, 'But I don't think God could hear me.' I shared her feelings and yet the experience on the fire escape some thirteen years earlier had never left me. The Holman Hunt painting certainly didn't have a flip side showing Jesus storming back out through the door! He doesn't go back on his word. I wouldn't go back on mine. I tried to remain faithful but so often it was just too hard and I appreciated the wise and kind people who took the burden and said, 'Don't you worry. We'll do the praying for you.' There was no medical or visible reason for confidence, or even much hope, yet many friends persevered in prayer and faith. God had indicated to a number of them that he had the timing of everything in his hand and this was borne out when Canon Jim Glennon, an Australian Anglican minister with a worldwide ministry of healing, just 'happened' to be visiting London. I had been brought out of the Intensive Care Unit and as I lay curled up in a contorted ball this quiet gentle man asked if he could pray for me. Very simply and with quiet authority he began to pray that my twisted body would be healed. I remember so little about him leaving; I know I fell into a deep sleep. A short time later I woke up and instantly felt able to sit up. I *knew* I could sit up. Yet previously it had taken two people to sit me forward to take a drink.

This was the start of a very rapid recovery, a physical restoration of muscles and limbs that was followed by a healing of the heart. I hadn't really realised that for years I had held a deep resentment towards the young man who had dropped me when I was training to be a ballet dancer. The cutting back of the brambles also involved a forgiveness for all that had happened. A conscious decision to forgive. And be forgiven. The handing back to God of all the negative to be used for his glory. That same flood of peace and wonder swept through the broken dreams and ambitions until the tide rose to an overflowing river of praise and healing that far surpassed the physical restoration.

One of my daughter's favourite verses from the Bible is, 'The eternal God is your refuge, and underneath are the everlasting arms' (Deuteronomy 33:27). As a family we have grown to depend on such promises as sometimes the waves of life seem set to build up and destroy. As a child I grew up in Devon where we spent a great deal of time on the beach. When we were satisfied with our freshly built sandcastles we would take our old-fashioned red metal spades and go on a search for seaweed, shells and used lollypop sticks with which to decorate our constructions. The metal spades were particularly effective for 'limpet removal'. There were enormous barnacled limpets covering many of the rocks and we devised horrible ways to prise these suckers off. It was worth all the effort as a row of limpet shells made a very realistic turret.

But so it has been with the enemy of life who has tried every conceivable way and trick to prise us away from God, away from his refuge and his everlasting arms. Since taking that wonderful decision, as a teenager, to follow Jesus I have endeavoured to keep close to him, to seek his face, to learn about his ways and teaching, to receive his gifts and pass them on. Within this deep desire to follow him there have been numerous occasions when the wrenching of the spade has caused misery and pain and the *only* thing I can rely on are his everlasting arms. The latest assault has been on our youngest daughter who was diagnosed with a malignant brain tumour at the age of ten years. This wave has threatened to engulf us all. Yet my personal and spiritual hopes for the future remain firm. While I have breath I will speak of his wonders, love and healing, but just a day at a time. The words of my grandfather help to keep a balance in my desire for more people to know Jesus: 'Stand aside, you bishops, and let the ordinary man get a glimpse of the man of Galilee!' I hope to never stand in the way or obscure anyone's view of Jesus but that through all our experiences, good and bad, I might help draw others also to:

> Turn your eyes upon Jesus,
> Look full in his wonderful face,
> And the things of earth will grow strangely dim
> In the light of his glory and grace.

It was the best decision I ever made to follow that face and look into those eyes of love and truth. Jesus has been like a firm and solid rock and foundation amidst much sickness and confusion, and has given us so much love through other people.

Without his glory and grace, I think sitting in the clearing of the rhododendron bushes would have been a lonely place.

12

Listening to God

R. T. Kendall

The best decision I ever made paved the way for making pivotal decisions throughout my life – none of which I regret. It began on 5 April 1942. I was six and a half years old. It was Easter Sunday morning. I told my parents that I wanted to become a Christian. I have no idea why I did this. It is possible that being Easter had something to do with it. I only know it was my own idea, because my dad immediately turned to my mother and said, 'Let's pray with R. T. now, why wait until we get to church?' I remember it as if it were yesterday; I knelt at my parents' bed alongside them and asked God to forgive my sins for Jesus's sake and come into my heart.

This means that virtually all my life I have been a Christian. I cannot imagine what it is like not to be brought up in a Christian home. I admit that, though, I became a Christian at such an early age that I later resented having to go to church every time the door opened. But my rebellion was minimal. I was basically a compliant child. I now realise how good God was in giving me the parents I had, not to mention his sovereign call on me when I was so young. But, as I said, this paved the way for my making life-changing decisions across the years. I want to mention some of them.

My call to preach

I used to want to be a trial lawyer. Although I had a prayer life as a teenager that would put most ministers to shame, I had been severely warned never to go into the ministry unless God called me. Whether my pastor had heard the famous words of Charles Spurgeon, 'If you can do anything else, do it' - I don't know. I can only recall being afraid to claim I was called to preach when I wasn't.

Back in my home in Kentucky there were many stories of men who had rather supernatural calls to preach. One of them was out in a field ploughing corn and he saw a cloud formation in the sky in the shape of the letters 'PC'. He interpreted that to mean 'Preach Christ', and started preaching. However, there were not a few who were convinced that God did indeed give the letters PC - but they really meant 'Plough Corn'!

In November 1954 a Scottish minister, John Sutherland Logan, came to Trevecca Nazarene College in Nashville, Tennessee, where I was a student. When he preached I was convinced I had just heard the greatest preaching ever. I approached him and asked him, 'How does one know he is called to preach?'

The truth is, I was wanting to be - which worried me more; I feared I would be getting a local call rather than one of long distance. Dr Logan kindly gave time. One day he said, 'You are called' - just like that.

I said, 'How do you know?'

He replied, 'Because you are.' He hemmed me into a corner in such a way that I could see for myself that I was truly called to preach. But I was so disappointed. No vision in the sky. No voice from Michael the Archangel - just a Scottish preacher. But I never looked back and never regretted the decision to go into the preaching ministry.

My return to academic life

I have passed over many crucial eras, such as: my 'Damascus Road' experience in my car (31 October 1955) which changed my outlook, theology and ecclesiastical career; my marriage to Louise on 28 June 1958; and my era of selling vacuum cleaners before becoming a Southern Baptist. After becoming the pastor of the Lauderdale Manors Baptist Church in Fort Lauderdale, Florida, I began to see the folly of not going to theological seminary as most other pastors did. Not only that; I feared having to live with myself down the road if I swept under the carpet the duty of submitting to further training.

But I still needed to know for sure that this was right. I found myself high up in a gallery in a church in Denver, Colorado, during the time of the Southern Baptist Convention (June 1970). The feeling of having to give up my church in Fort Lauderdale, where we were happy and secure, was scary. Furthermore, since I already knew theology fairly well – and had a reasonably good preaching gift, why should I wipe out several years of my life to learn academic things that (I thought) would bear no relevance on my preaching? I reckoned that, if I gave up my church and went to seminary or university, I would be forty before I would be finished with such education.

I relate the following reluctantly, for this could lead some people to use as a method what in fact can be dangerous. High up in that gallery I felt I was at the crossroads. I reached in my pocket for my little New Testament. 'Lord,' I said, 'if you want me to leave my church and return to academic life, there is a passage in this little Bible that can tell me this is your idea.' My heart was pounding hard. I opened my Bible and my eyes fell on Acts 7:22-3 (AV): 'And Moses was learned in all the wisdom of the Egyptians, and was mighty in words and in deeds. And when he was forty years old, it came into his heart to visit his brothers the children of Israel.'

That verse met head-on my two big questions. First, what if I spend time learning things that are not related to my gospel ('wisdom of the Egyptians') and second, what if I don't get back into the full-time ministry until I am forty ('when he was full forty years old')? I never looked back. It eventually led us to Oxford in September 1973.

My learning to forgive

After completing my research at Oxford I began my ministry at Westminster Chapel on 1 February 1977. Arguably this paralleled the greatest and most important decision of my life. But something was to take place that, as far as my spiritual pilgrimage is concerned, outweighs nearly every decision I've ever made. Indeed, what follows almost certainly *is* the best decision I have made: forgiving those who hurt me.

When I began my ministry at Westminster Chapel I thought that, at long last, I had been adequately prepared for this new ministry. At the academic level I had a B.A., two Masters degrees and a degree in theology from Oxford. So I thought to myself, 'I'm ready.'

God then looked down from heaven at me with a concerned smile and said, 'Really?' Little did I know that my greatest preparation lay ahead. I knew that C. H. Spurgeon once said, 'If I knew I had twenty-five years left to live, I'd spend twenty of them in preparation.' But I had no idea that God would put that on me! The Greek word in Hebrews 12:6 translated 'chasteneth' (AV) or 'disciplines' (NIV) literally means 'enforced learning'. It is when God as it were puts a pistol to our heads to get our attention. In my case, this kind of preparation was rougher than any work done at an academic level. And far more important.

I blush to think that I had taken little notice of the idea of forgiving your enemies over the years. That the 'Lord's Prayer' with the petition 'Forgive us our trespasses, as we forgive those who have trespassed against us', made a liar out of me thousands of times did not faze me. 'We all sin,' I said to myself. 'Nobody's perfect.' And yet God blessed me in spite of this and used me across the years. He is so gracious. Little did I know that I was earmarked to be dealt with on a fundamental issue at the right juncture, and it came unexpectedly.

I cannot give the date, lest there be those who might try to pinpoint the exact event and persons referred to. I can only say it was at the height of my greatest trial at the time and the result was my self-justifying feelings of resentment, bitterness and self-pity. I could talk about it to no one, only my wife.

But during this time an old friend, Josif Tson of Romania, was passing through London and asked to see me. Little did I know this would be the most life-changing event of my life. I decided to bring up my hurt. Since he was from outside London (and nobody would know) I told him what 'they' did to me. I poured my heart out and told him all I could think of. 'Is there anything more?' he asked.

'No, that's it,' I said.

Josif asked for fifteen minutes to take a brief nap and hoped I'd have a cup of tea ready for him. The tea had been brewing for much of that time. When he returned and took a sip he said, 'Now that is what I call a cup of tea!' Then he looked at me and kindly pointed his right index finger between my eyes.

'R. T.,' he began firmly in his lovely Romanian accent, 'You must totally forgeeve them. Until you *totally* forgeeve them you will be in chains. Release them and you will be released.'

Nobody had ever talked like that to me in my life. 'Faithful are the wounds of a friend' (Proverbs 27:69, AV) comes to mind when I reflect on that moment.

'Josif, I just remembered something else I hadn't told you.' He wasn't interested in more of my self-pity.

'R. T., you must totally forgeeve them. Release them and you will be released.'

'Josif, I can't.'

'You can and you must,' he replied. I was hemmed in. It was

my biggest test – the hardest thing I've ever had to do. But I did it. Or so I thought.

What happened was this. When I did it (that is, in my heart – I never went to anyone and said, 'I now totally forgive you for what you did'), a wonderful peace came over me. Clear thinking. The presence of Jesus. The ungrieved Holy Spirit welled up inside. Then I *remembered what they did* and the resentment returned. The peace vanished. Muddled thinking emerged. The Lord Jesus was not real and there was no sense of the presence of the Holy Spirit.

I began to realise how impoverished I was by being bitter. I was losing fast every time I began to dwell on 'what they did' to me. When I would begin to forgive again, the peace would come back; when I became bitter, the peace left. Simple mathematics – putting two and two together – told me that I was being stupid to withhold forgiveness. Josif was right – I was in chains; when I released them, I was released.

The big mistake people make is thinking we are hurting those who injured us by not forgiving them. 'Fear has to do with punishment' (1 John 4:18). We want to punish them and we think that by not forgiving them they are getting what they deserve. If we take another by surprise and say, 'I forgive you', it is often an opportunity to stick the knife in – which shows we haven't forgiven them at all! We want to punish because of fear in us. Total forgiveness reflects love, casts out fear. The devil's big lie is that we are giving them a dose of what's coming to them when we hold a grudge. The truth is, we are set free and enriched beyond measure when we actually totally forgive.

It is my own experience combined with many years of pastoral experience that 90 per cent of those we have to forgive (even if we put them under a lie detector) *sincerely don't think they've done anything* to be forgiven of! Naive people often think they will put the record straight by going to the person and saying, 'I forgive you for what you did.' Do *that* and you've got real trouble on your hands! They will bristle and say, 'Really? For what? What have I done?" It only makes things a thousand times worse.

Forgiveness must be in the heart. I have yet to go to anyone who hurt me and say, 'I forgive you.' In every case I have had to deal with it internally. If they come to me and say, 'I'm sorry', that is wonderful. It rarely happens. I can't afford to wait for that sublime moment. Life goes on, it is too short, and I must be absolutely sure I am devoid of any trace of bitterness, resentment or self-pity.

How do I know I have totally forgiven another person? The answers are supplied in the life of Joseph. I have elaborated on this in my book *God Meant It for Good* (which I dedicated to Josif Tson). First, tell nobody 'what they did'. You protect the identity or identities of those who hurt you. Why? Paul said, 'Be kind and compassionate to one another, forgiving each other, just as in Christ God forgave you' (Ephesians 4:32). God will not tell you what he knows about me (a lot – I thank God you will never know!). I therefore tell nobody what I know about another. You will say, 'But you told Josif Tson.' True, but not to turn Josif against anybody; I was needing help – and I got it!

Second, we must not let those who have hurt us be afraid of us. We want them to fear and be intimidated for one reason: to punish them. If I want them to be afraid of me, I have not totally forgiven them.

Third, do not send another on a guilt trip or allow the person to be angry with himself or herself. Joseph said to his astonished brothers, 'Do not be angry with yourselves for selling me here' (Genesis 45:5). If I say to you, 'I forgive you but I hope you feel pretty bad about it', I am wanting you to feel punished. When God forgives us, he wants us to forgive ourselves (1 John 1:9).

Fourth, let the other person save face. Do you want to turn an enemy into a friend forever? Let him or her save face. Joseph presented to his brothers total forgiveness on a silver platter when he said, 'It was not you who sent me here, but God' (Genesis 45:8). That seemed to be too good to be true. But it was true.

Fifth, assure them that their greatest fear will never be fulfilled.

Joseph's brothers' greatest fear was that Jacob, their father, would find out what his jealous sons had done. Joseph instructed them what they were to say to their father and it is carefully worded by what they were *not* to say, namely, what they did to him (Genesis 45:9–13). You can blackmail a person and keep him in agony by such a threat.

Sixth, you keep on doing it. Seventeen years later Joseph showed that his forgiveness was *total*; he continued to do it after Jacob died (Genesis 50:20). Total forgiveness is a life sentence – you do it, daily, as long as you live.

Finally, you pray for them – as Jesus did (Luke 23:34). Jesus did not say, 'I forgive you', but 'Father, *you* forgive them.' This means intercession on their behalf – that they will get away with what they did – and be blessed.

It's not easy. It was my biggest test. But it paved the way for more pivotal decisions. Had I not learned to forgive, God would have put me out of the ministry. But because I learned to forgive, I found that a wonderful fringe benefit was hearing the voice of the Holy Spirit more clearly than I had ever known.

Listening to God

As I write these lines there have been three epoch-making decisions for us at Westminster Chapel. The first was inviting Arthur Blessitt to the Chapel. The man who was in a sense the father of the 'Jesus Movement' in the 1960s – who began a coffee-house ministry in Hollywood's Sunset Strip – took the large wooden cross down from the wall of his coffee house and began carrying it around the world. Arthur is now in the *Guinness Book of Records* for the longest walk of any human being in history. He has exceeded the agenda of walking around the earth and has made it across 170 countries – which I believe is the sum total of every nation – of the world. Arthur has met many heads of state. He spent days with Yasser Arafat, stayed in Israel's Prime Minister Begin's home, was awarded the Sinai Peace

Medal. On top of that he is a wonderful communicator.

My motive for inviting Arthur was to get close to him. I regarded him as the most like Jesus of any person I had met. He agreed to preach for us, but I wasn't prepared for what he insisted on doing – three things: he gave an appeal after each time he preached (unthinkable then at Westminster Chapel); he got us singing choruses (the chandeliers fell); and he got us out on the streets talking to total strangers about Jesus (which I never did in my life). Arthur turned us upside down. I nearly lost my job a year or two later, but we survived. We were never to be quite the same again. From the Chapel's point of view, it was my greatest decision. Arthur was the earthquake that rolled the stone away.

Second, bringing Paul Cain into Westminster Chapel. When I first heard of this man I thought he was occultic. To me, anybody who calls out people's names and addresses and dates of birth smacks of the devil – pure and simple. I was wary. The details of my friendship with Paul Cain cannot be told here. But once I was convinced he was a man of God (with a gift that seems an awful lot like Samuel's or Elijah's to me), it became significant for all of us in my church. It opened us up to the prophetic. We never before took seriously anything like this. My feeling was, 'The Bible is enough.' But I began to recall Dr Martyn Lloyd-Jones's words to me: 'The Bible was not given to replace divine revelation; it was given to correct abuses.'

Paul Cain has done our church no harm. His gift has even spared us of a church split. He has blessed a number of our members. He prophesied of my wife Louise's ministry to the deaf, which is now flourishing. His sermon on 'worship' moved us further than ever – a separate story in itself. He prepared us for what was to come in 1994, sharing with our deacons two years before that 'Isaac will be an ugly baby', which I will explain below.

I come now to a third eventful moment for me during my ministry at Westminster Chapel: taking on the 'Toronto

Blessing', as it was called. In May 1994 I led my church to adopt a prayer covenant that includes four petitions, and which we pray literally every day. The third petition is this: 'We pray for the manifestation of the glory of God in our midst *along with* an ever-increasing *openness in us* to the manner in which you choose to manifest that glory.' Why this? First, the only manifestation we care about is the manifestation of the Lord's glory. We want nothing else. But I also saw that God might not choose to manifest his glory precisely as he did yesterday. I'd be happy if he did. I could live with the 'glory' I saw in the early Nazarenes. I could live with what I believe to be true about the Welsh revival 1904–05. But God may or may not accommodate us with what coheres with our comfort zone. Hence we pray as much for ourselves to be *open* to God's sovereign choice as to how he may wish to manifest his glory as we do for that unveiling itself.

Four days after we had the new Prayer Covenant cards printed up, my friends Lyndon Bowring and Charlie Colchester joined me for an evening in London's West End. Just before we went to see *Schindler's List* we went to a Chinese restaurant in Gerrard Street. While waiting for our food Charlie spoke up, 'Have you guys heard about this Toronto thing?' Neither of us had a clue what he was talking about. He began to describe how at his church, Holy Trinity, Brompton, people were being prayed for after the service and then falling to the floor in laughter. Lyndon and I looked at each other, rolled our eyes heavenward, and listened as Charlie was clearly gripped by what had been happening. He asked, 'Do you think this could be of God?' I replied that if you put me under a lie detector I would say it was *not* of God. We finished our meal and went to the cinema, but I found myself thinking of that conversation even more than the unforgettable film we saw.

I unveiled our new Prayer Covenant publicly the following Sunday. When I explained the implications of the third petition – the prayer for the manifestation of God's glory and our being open to the manner in which he chose to manifest that glory – I referred to the Toronto phenomenon. I stated that I did not believe it was of God *but* one must always be open to the unusual things like this since church history has taught us God *can* surprise us with the unusual and unprecedented. In any case I had gone on 'public record that this particular phenomenon was not of God.

A few days later a ministers' meeting was being held on the Chapel premises. Lyndon Bowring introduced me to Bob Cheeseman who had recently returned from Toronto. Bob's face was beaming. His life had been dramatically changed, he said. I invited him to come to the vestry and pray for me. I was unconvinced but still felt I had to be open. In the meantime a close friend had turned up to have coffee with me in my vestry. I explained to him that I had just invited a man who had just returned from Toronto to pray for me. 'You've heard about Toronto,' I assumed. He hadn't. I quickly explained what I knew about it. He is a fellow minister of reformed views who was about as interested in what I just described as I might be in toe dancing on ice. Seconds later there was a knock on the door, Bob came in. The two ministers already knew each other and obviously had mutual respect for each other. I explained that Bob was going to pray for me and that the other man could look on. 'He can pray for me too,' my friend said courteously. As we stood to pray there was another knock on the door. Gerald Coates had come to say hello.

I said, 'Bob is just getting ready to pray for me.'

Gerald replied, 'I want in on this.' So now four of us were praying. They were praying for me. But, as best as I can recall, not ten seconds elapsed before my friend fell forwards – right on the floor of my vestry, face down. I gulped and swallowed hard.

'I am impressed, I must admit,' I said nervously. Ten minutes later the *three* of them commenced praying for me. Nothing happened. But that was the moment I was forced to reassess my opinion.

A few days later Ken Costa, Church Warden at Holy Trinity,

Brompton, phoned. 'Something unusual has happened at our church and I was wondering if you have written anything on 1 John 4:1–4' – a passage that discusses testing the spirits and distinguishing false prophets from true. He sent a courier immediately to fetch tapes of four sermons I had preached from that passage. He took me to lunch soon afterwards to discuss what was going on at HTB. By the time lunch was over I knew in my heart I had been on the wrong side of something God was in. I could see myself in the succession of those who opposed Edwards, Whitefield, Wesley and the Welsh Revival. I said to my wife Louise after that lunch, 'I am going to have to climb down.' I shared the same with my deacons that Friday evening.

The following Sunday, just before my morning prayer, I made a public climb-down on Toronto. 'How many times have you heard me say over the years, "What if Revival broke out at All Souls, Langham Place; or Kensington Temple? Would we be willing to affirm it even though it wasn't here at Westminster Chapel?" ' (Mind you, I never thought I'd have to do that.) On that morning I affirmed that God was at work at HTB and we prayed publicly for Sandy Millar, their vicar and my friend.

In December 1994 Colin Dye of London's Kensington Temple asked me if I'd like to meet Rodney Howard-Browne. Yes. I knew that the Toronto phenomenon was traceable to Rodney – the falling down, the laughter. But I was expecting no more than to meet him. As soon as I met him I sensed that across from the breakfast table was a guileless man of God. 'Baby Isaac,' I kept thinking. 'Baby Isaac.' In October 1992 Paul Cain and I had held the first 'Word and Spirit' conference at Wembley. Graham Kendrick wrote a hymn for us, 'Jesus restore to us again', which demonstrated the need for the Word and the Spirit to come together. I preached a sermon that amounted to a prophetic statement: as Abraham sincerely believed that Ishmael was the promised child, so many have assumed that the charismatic renewal *was* the revival the church had been praying for. Wrong, I said. Isaac is coming. What God is going to do ahead will be a hundred times greater than anything the church has yet seen. It will be as proportionately greater as the promise contained in Isaac was greater than that which pertained to Ishmael. It offended charismatics because they felt I was calling all of them Ishmael; it offended evangelicals partly because I affirmed the charismatic renewal as something God was in (for there was a place for Ishmael in God's sovereign plan).

I knew little about Rodney Howard-Browne. All I know is, 'Baby Isaac' kept coming to me as I looked at him across the breakfast table. I also remembered a word Paul Cain gave to our deacons in March 1993: 'Isaac will be an ugly baby. He will look like Ishmael, he will burp like Ishmael, he will have to have diapers changed like Ishmael. But as an ugly baby sometimes turns out to be a beautiful person, so Isaac will be the most handsome person ever.' Baby Isaac. Isaac means 'laughter'. I did not know then that Rodney himself had always seen his own ministry as unstopping wells – the only thing Isaac ever really did (see Genesis 26:18-32). Rodney's main verse – which he quotes so often when he preaches – is John 7:38: 'Out of his belly shall flow rivers of living water' (AV). I did not know this either. But I now know that the thrust of his ministry, giving joy and laughter by the laying on of hands, he bases on John 7:38. The origin of the joy and laughter is from within a person. Rodney's ministry is to *unstop the well* – that the joy will flow.

I hadn't heard Rodney preach but I asked him if he would be prepared to stop by my church the following Saturday morning. Why? I wanted him to stand in my pulpit and pray (I had done the same thing with Paul Cain), then I wanted him to pray for my wife Louise. He arrived the next Saturday, then went up to the pulpit and prayed aloud in the empty auditorium. Rodney did not pray spontaneously but *read* a prayer that actually emerged from the Welsh Revival. We returned to the vestry for him to pray for my wife.

Louise had been in a severe depression for five years or more. At one stage it was so awful that I thought I'd have to give up my ministry and return to America. Parallel with the depression she developed a bad cough. Her GP sent her to the Royal Brompton Hospital; we feared the worst. The cough became so severe that often she could not sleep a night through without having to get up for a couple of hours. She also developed an eye condition – seeing flashing lights in her peripheral vision – and was advised to go to the casualty department at St Thomas's Hospital. The consultant warned her that the cough could result in a detached retina. Rodney and his wife Adonica prayed for Louise for about five minutes. She was instantly healed. That was in December 1994. In January 1995 she spent a week at Rodney's meetings in Lakeland, Florida. 'It's the nearest you get to heaven without dying,' she said to me on the phone from Lakeland. She returned to London transformed. Our son T. R. got in on this and his life too was turned upside down.

Our son T. R. (Robert Tillman II – we call him T. R.) was living in the Florida Keys when Louise went over to Lakeland. He had planned only to take her to his home but came a day early at her insistence. He was not the slightest bit interested in the sort of thing Rodney emphasised, but agreed to stay only for an hour or two. Before the evening was over he was taken up by a ministry he had never seen before. A month later he went to New Orleans to hear Rodney and was touched by the Spirit in a very, very powerful way. Paul Cain always said that our son T. R. needed to see 'life after life', and Rodney's ministry did that for him. This means that Rodney's ministry had touched two out of four of our family!

All the above paved the way for where we are now. I have no idea what God will do next in my life, or in the life of Westminster Chapel; for in recent years these two have become almost interchangeable. I have made some mistakes during my time in Westminster, but they don't include any decision described above. I give God all the praise for the presence of mind that I've had. It began at Easter 1942.

A Survival Guide to Frontline Living

Sarah de Carvalho

How can I discover my calling and follow it faithfully?

A *Survival Guide to Frontline Living* is a unique handbook for all Christians called by God to devote their lives to his service. We may be called to the mission field or to the family home, to work in a high-street business or on the factory floor – whatever the calling, it is rarely an easy ride. If we follow God, we are likely to face physical and spiritual obstacles which, without faith, seem insurmountable.

Sarah de Carvalho speaks from dramatic personal experience of the spiritual frontline having given up her glittering, well-paid media career to live among and care for street children in Brazil. This book is packed with powerful, practical, biblical advice for all those considering work on the frontline, and updates the story of Sarah's first book, *The Street Children of Brazil – One Woman's Remarkable Story*.

Hodder & Stoughton
0 340 74545 2

Rainbows Through the Rain

Fiona Castle

Fiona Castle has known the depths of grief and loneliness which bereavement brings. But she also knows faith and hope and that it is possible to come out safely on the other side, changed but also strengthened. This wonderful anthology shares her sources of inspiration with us: readings, poems and hymns from the past and present, including her own thoughts and poetry.

This is a treasure to dip into or to give as a gift.

Hodder & Stoughton
0 340 70980 4

Is God Good for Women?

Michele Guinness

Does God have a down on women? Anyone who judges his personal preferences by the history of religion could be forgiven for thinking that he does.

Traditionally religious institutions do not seem good for women. They have tended to side with the status quo which keeps women in their place, dutiful, domestic and dependent; yet many of the pioneers who have risen to the challenge, who have dared to excel in a male world, have done so because of, not in spite of, their faith.

In this book, which became a personal pilgrimage, Michele Guinness has talked to a number of women who have broken new ground in very different ways and this is a fascinating and inspiring collection. We meet a rabbi, a police superintendent and a chief executive among others as they reflect on similar issues including career and celibacy, marriage and motherhood, ambition and power.

Hodder & Stoughton
0 340 67870 4

To Know and Serve God
– A Biography of James I. Packer

Alister McGrath

James Packer is one of the best-known names in the modern Christian world. *Christianity Today* readers named him one of the most influential theologians of the twentieth century, second only to C. S. Lewis. His books have sold more than two million copies worldwide, and are cited by many who have read them as marking turning points in their lives as Christians. His rare combination of theological competence and spiritual wisdom places him alongside the great spiritual writers of the evangelical tradition such as John Owen, Richard Baxter, George Whitefield and Jonathan Edwards.

Alister McGrath's magnificent biography, written with the full co-operation of James Packer, tells the story of this great thinker and, by doing so, casts light on the remarkable growth of evangelicalism in the last generation.

Hodder & Stoughton
0 340 55671 4

The Anointing
R. T. Kendall

Do you have a fear of being a 'has-been'? Although many of us long
to be blessed by the anointing of the Holy Spirit, R. T. Kendall believes
it is possible to abuse this anointing – and to become yesterday's man
or woman. This happens by trying to move outside our calling and
capabilities, for example, or even through impatience.

Are you frustrated that your gift has not been recognised?
R. T. says your moment will come! But you may have to suffer the
pain of being tomorrow's man or woman – being misunderstood or
ignored in the meantime.

Drawing on the Bible, especially the lives of Saul, Samuel and
David, as well as on his own experience, R. T. helps to identify our
current usefulness and urges us to seek a fresh anointing of the
Holy Spirit each day.

Hodder & Stoughton
0 340 72144 8

The Thorn in the Flesh
R. T. Kendall

In Corinthians 12:7 Paul makes the extraordinary admission that
*'to keep me from becoming conceited because of these surpassingly
great revelations, there was given me a thorn in my flesh, a messenger
of Satan, to torment me'*.

Although we can never be sure what that torment was, many of us will
know what it is to be afflicted with a 'thorn in the flesh', a painful
and chronic problem which does not seem to go away.

In this book, R. T. Kendall explains what a thorn in the flesh is, why
we have it and what we should understand by it. Looking with
compassion at the kinds of acute situation in which we may find
ourselves in everyday life, he shows us how the grace of God
is sufficient for us whatever our thorn, and how it can lead
us into unimaginable intimacy with Jesus.

Hodder & Stoughton
0 340 74546 0

Amateurs Series

Bible Reading for Amateurs

Michael Green

How to approach and read the Bible is a puzzle to many of us.

The Bible is the world's bestseller but how can we get the most out of its teaching and what relevance does it have for us today? This easy-to-read guide shows us that throughout the Bible God is revealing himself to us and directing our lives. It is a life-changing book.

Bible Reading for Amateurs clearly shows us how to approach the Bible and takes us step-by-step through how we can learn to enjoy reading and reflecting upon the Bible by ourselves or in a group.

Hodder & Stoughton
0 340 77454 1

Evangelism for Amateurs

Michael Green

Evangelism makes most of us feel totally inadequate.

We simply feel like running for cover: the last thing we want to be seen as is mindless enthusiasts pushing our views on other people. But if we are to follow Jesus's command to go and make disciples, it isn't something we can just ignore.

Evangelism for Amateurs is full of ideas on reaching out to our families, friends and neighbours in a way that is relaxed, 'human' and possible, even to those of us who feel unqualified for the job. Rather than 'hijacking' people with the gospel, we can confidently begin to help them find a living faith for themselves.

Hodder & Stoughton
0 340 71420 4

Theology for Amateurs

Alister McGrath

Many of us find theology difficult or irrelevant.

Written clearly and simply by one of the world's best-known and respected theologians, this book shows how theology can actually add new depth to our faith.

Many Christians have only scratched the surface of the gospel. *Theology for Amateurs* shows us how to go deeper. Theology can strengthen our personal faith, stimulate our minds and enrich our worship. Theology brings our minds and hearts together, and sets them on fire with wonder and amazement.

Hodder & Stoughton
0 340 74553 3